instant maths ideas
FOR KEY STAGE 3 TEACHERS

data, numeracy and ICT

Colin Foster

T

Introduction

Teachers are busy people, so I'll be brief.
Let me tell you what this book *isn't*.

- It *isn't* a book you have to make time to read; it's a book that will *save* you time.
  Take it into the classroom and use ideas from it straight away.
  Anything requiring preparation or equipment (e.g., photocopies, scissors, an overhead projector, etc.) begins with the word "**NEED**" in bold followed by the details.

- It *isn't* a scheme of work, and it isn't even arranged by age or pupil "level".
  Many of the ideas can be used equally well with pupils at different ages and stages.
  Instead the items are simply arranged by topic.
  (There is, however, an index at the back linking the "key objectives" from the *Key Stage 3 Framework* to the sections in these three volumes.)
  The three volumes cover ***Number and Algebra*** (1), ***Shape and Space*** (2) and ***Data, Numeracy and ICT*** (3).

- It *isn't* a book of exercises or worksheets.
  Although you're welcome to photocopy anything you wish, photocopying is expensive and very little here needs to be photocopied for pupils. Most of the material is intended to be presented by the teacher orally or on the board.
  Answers and comments are given on the right side of most of the pages or sometimes on separate pages as explained.

This is a book to make notes in. Cross out anything you don't like or would never use. Add in your own ideas or references to other resources. Put "8R" (for example) next to anything you use with that class if you want to remember that you've used it with them.

Some of the material in this book will be familiar to many teachers, and I'd like to thank everyone whose ideas I've included. I'm particularly grateful to those people who have discussed some of these ideas with me; especially Keith Proffitt, Paul Andrews, John Cooper and Simon Wadsley. Special thanks go to Graham Foster for expert computer behaviour management!

Colin Foster
July 2003

© Colin Foster, 2003.

Contents

Volume 3 – Data, Numeracy and ICT

3.1	**Collecting Data**	*4*
3.2	**Presenting Data Graphically**	*10*
3.3	**Statistical Calculations**	*14*
3.4	**Combinations**	*23*
3.5	**Probability**	*27*
3.6	**Numeracy Ideas**	*43*
3.7	**Spreadsheet Tasks**	*73*
3.8	**LOGO Tasks**	*80*
	Mathematics Books and Websites	*83*
	Key Stage 3 Strategy – **Key Objectives Index**	*84*

3.1 Collecting Data

- The first stage is always to decide on a *hypothesis*. Everything from then on is geared to testing the hypothesis. We probably won't "prove" or "disprove" it completely, but we'll get strong/weak evidence in favour of or against it. A hypothesis is a *statement*, not a question or a "title".
- Making a good plan before you start saves lots of time and wasted effort. Key questions to ask pupils are "How exactly are you going to do that?"; "What problems might you run into?"; "What might go wrong with that?"; "Why might that not be easy?"; "How long do you expect that part to take?", etc.
- An interesting hypothesis can make all the difference to pupils' motivation. Topical or local ideas work best so long as they're not so personal that they cause embarrassment. Ethics is obviously an issue, and relates to how the data is collected and to how it's used; anonymity, confidentiality, etc.
- Questionnaires can be fun to write, but if every pupil wants every other pupil to fill in a questionnaire then the photocopying costs will be astronomical! One workable strategy is to invent a questionnaire on the board as a class exercise containing all the questions people want answers to for testing their hypotheses. Everyone copies it down as we go (because the data will make no sense unless we remember the questions). Before the next lesson the teacher prepares a results table (A3, perhaps) with space for every pupil's answers, one pupil per line, and during the next lesson this is passed around the classroom while the pupils are doing some other task. Every pupil fills in his/her answers and then this sheet is photocopied (perhaps reduced to A4) and given to pupils, maybe one between two, for processing the data.

3.1.1 NEED "Skateboarding Questionnaire" sheet.

What makes for a good/bad questionnaire?

Choose a hypothesis and think of good and bad questions for a questionnaire.

A common error is to include the same value at the start of one tick-box range as is at the end of the previous one; e.g., "0-2", "2-4", etc. (Here it would not be clear which box to tick for "2".)

You can collect badly produced questionnaires written by "important" people/organisations, such as the deputy head, exam boards, or government departments!

Bad questions are
- *unclear;*
- *irrelevant;*
- *biased;*
- *embarrassing; or*
- *give results which are hard to interpret / process.*

Tips for good questions include these:
- *use tick boxes;*
- *specify ranges of values (get the "filler-in" to do the grouping of data so that we don't have to);*
- *remember to include "other", where applicable;*
- *if amounts are requested, state the units (e.g., years, cm, £, etc.).*

(You might need to conceal their origins to protect the guilty!)

3.1.2 Pupils write a questionnaire to test their own hypotheses.
Popular topics include sport, food (especially sweets), smoking, television, music, shops, leisure facilities, often comparing boys and girls.

You may need to be cautious about reinforcing stereotypes: a hypothesis may be a "prejudice".

This works best if the whole class discuss what makes a good hypothesis and what makes a good questionnaire before pupils work independently on this.

You will need to be alert to hypotheses that can be tested by asking one simple question; e.g., "Most pupils think that school uniform should be abolished" could lead to a rather short "questionnaire", so the pupil could develop an additional hypothesis or make this one a bit more nuanced.

3.1.3 **NEED** photocopies of a page of text from two different books (aimed at different age pupils): novels may be best.

This book is aimed at year 6 (say) and this one at year 8 (say). How would you expect them to be different?
Which of these ideas could we test using statistics? Can you suggest a suitable hypothesis?

e.g., "Books aimed at older pupils will have, on average, longer words."

Exactly what would we have to do to test this hypothesis?

100 words from each text may be a sensible sample size.

You can begin by discussing what might be a suitable hypothesis.

The book aimed at older people might be expected to have a more complex storyline, more mature themes, longer words, harder words, smaller print, more pages, be more expensive, etc.

Write the ideas on the board. It may be best to agree on one hypothesis to pursue, or different pupils or groups of pupils could work on different hypotheses.

Pupils need to work out a clear step-by-step plan before they start, dealing with questions such as "how many words will you include in your sample?", "how will you choose them?", "what will you do about hyphenated words?", etc.

3.1.4 Methods of Travel to School.
This well-worn idea can still be of interest provided that there is a hypothesis and some clear purpose to the survey.
e.g., "Is it true that people nowadays are walking less and driving more?";
"A politician claims that nationally most children still travel the main part of their journey to school on foot. Is that true for this class?"

What should we do about people who use a variety of means to get to school or come different ways on different days?

A more complicated type of hypothesis would be "Most people in this class took less than 20 minutes to get to school this morning."

Why is walking less popular than it once was? safety concerns, too busy, live further from school than people used to, etc.

*What are the advantages of walking?
healthy (but is it if the air is full of vehicle fumes?), sociable, no traffic/parking problems, cheap, independent, etc.*

There are several possible approaches; e.g., "What was the main method you used to get to school this morning?" (Remember to include "other" in case someone rode in by horse or landed by helicopter!)

You could group the data (e.g., 1-10, 11-20, 21-30 min, etc.) and draw a bar chart. It may be better to ask people to tick a range for how long it took rather than simply to offer either "< 20" or "≥ 20", because you could then use the same data to test a similar hypothesis (< 10 mins, say).

3.1.5 **NEED** stopwatches (you could perhaps borrow some from the Science department).
Do something and time how long it takes;
e.g.,
- saying the alphabet backwards;
- estimating 1 minute: with eyes closed (so that clocks/other pupils aren't an influence) pupils face a clock with a seconds hand (perhaps held by the teacher). They open their eyes when they think 1 minute is up and write down the time showing on the clock;
- doing a tangram (or similar) puzzle;
- putting a list of names into alphabetical order.

These are relatively quick and easy ways of getting some continuous data to use for testing a hypothesis.

This list could easily be extended.

3.1.6 Subtleties of Sampling.
Imagine I stand on a motorway bridge and have some way of measuring the speeds of the vehicles on the motorway (say I borrow a radar gun from the police). Imagine I count the number of vehicles that go under the bridge in one direction (assume the motorway isn't too busy) and I keep a record of the number of *speeding* vehicles.
Say 20% of the vehicles are breaking the speed limit. Is that a valid test?

There are lots of factors to consider; e.g., is this a typical road?, did I sample enough vehicles?, was it during "rush hour"?, etc. But also, the sampling method is actually biased, because if you stand in a stationary place you are more likely to be passed by a speeding vehicle than a slower one, because they are travelling faster. You inevitably over-sample the faster vehicles by the method of sampling. (Imagine that throughout the motorway there were lots of cars all going at 5 mph – it's quite unlikely one will pass under your bridge during the time you're doing your counting.)

3.1.7 **NEED** photocopy of A and B lines (see sheet) – or you can use two readily available lengths; e.g., length of classroom and width of exercise book. Estimate the lengths of the two lines to the nearest mm. Write down in rough – you can't change your mind later!
Which length do you think we will estimate more accurately? (That's our hypothesis; e.g., "On average people are better at estimating short lengths than long lengths".)

Make a table on the board, beginning

length (to nearest mm)	frequency
0-9	

and going as far as necessary. (Different ranges may be needed, depending on the sizes of the lengths estimated.) Hands up for each group.
Check that total frequency is the same as the number of people in the room.

Ask pupils beforehand to put away rulers etc., and to close exercise books that contain squared paper. Emphasise that "estimate" just means "best guess" in this context.

People usually think that they can estimate the length of the shorter line better because they can more easily imagine dividing it into centimetres if it's only a few cm long.

*Draw grouped bar charts and/or frequency polygons and compare the distributions.
Is there any evidence to support our hypothesis? Can you estimate the true lengths of the lines from our data?*

Actual lengths: A is 53 mm; B is 128 mm.

People probably find it easiest to estimate "medium-sized" lengths that are within our common experience.

3.1.8 **NEED** rulers or metre sticks.
One route to continuous data is to measure "reaction times". It's best to find the mean of three attempts, discounting freak results ("I wasn't ready!").
One pupil holds the zero end of a ruler between two open fingers of another pupil and without warning drops the ruler. The other pupil catches the ruler as quickly as possible and the measured length is an indication of reaction time.

Typical values are around 0.1 to 0.3 seconds.

For what jobs might you need fast reaction times? What things would affect someone's reaction time, do you think?

*Hold the ruler over a bag or coat so that it isn't damaged by hitting the floor.
30 cm rulers may not be long enough!*

*Remember that long length indicates long reaction time (slow reactions), but the two are not proportional. If the length dropped is l cm, then the reaction time t (in seconds) is $t = \sqrt{\dfrac{l}{490}}$.
(Multiply by 1000 to convert to milliseconds.)*

aeroplane pilot, driving instructor, train driver, operator of machinery, zoo-keeper

tiredness, alcohol/drugs, stress, age

3.1.9 **NEED** tape measures or long rulers.
Is there any correlation between hand-span and arm length (wrist to elbow)?

(Of course, within any school year the range of different ages is likely to be almost 12 months and possibly more.)

These statistics are less problematic than height and weight, which are too sensitive for many pupils.

Generally there is reasonably strong correlation within a class of similar-age pupils.

Skateboarding Questionnaire

Here are two versions of a questionnaire about skateboarding.
The aim is to find out about pupils' attitudes to skateboarding at school.

What is different about the questionnaires?
Why do you think these pupils wrote the questionnaires the way they did?

Andy's questionnaire

1. Do you think that keeping healthy is important? Yes/No

2. Do you think that skateboarding is a good form of exercise? Yes/No

3. Do you think that the school should encourage pupils to do things that promote their health? Yes/No

4. Do you agree that there should be a skateboarding area at school? Yes/No

---

Billie's questionnaire

1. Do you think that keeping healthy is important? Yes/No

2. Do you think that skateboarding can be dangerous? Yes/No

3. Do you think that the school should discourage pupils from injuring themselves on pointless and dangerous activities? Yes/No

4. Do you agree that skateboarding should be banned at school? Yes/No

---

What makes these questionnaires biased?

Can you write a better version.

Can you make a version that other people agree is unbiased?

Sampling

- **Population**
  This refers to the whole set of data values (they don't have to be people to be a population).
  It has a mean μ (mu) and variance σ^2 (sigma squared), but the population is usually so big that it wouldn't be practicable to work these out exactly using every piece of data.
  So instead you take a **sample** and find the mean $\bar{x}$ and variance $\text{var}(x)$ of your sample and use these as estimates of μ and σ^2.

- **Sample**
  To give accurate answers, the sample you take must be
  ✓ **large enough**, so that your results aren't distorted by a few unusual values.
    The **sampling fraction** is a way of saying how big your sample is relative to the population:
    $$\text{sampling fraction} = \frac{\text{sample size}}{\text{population size}}$$

  ✓ **representative**, so that what's true of the sample is true of the population generally.
    This means having a fair way of choosing which values go into the sample.

- **Simple random sampling**
  Here, every possible sample of that size is equally likely to be chosen, and therefore every member of the population is just as likely to be picked.
  (Calculator random numbers are often useful.)

- **Stratified sampling**
  Use this when you expect there to be different sub-groups of the population (called **strata**) with *different* properties, so you want to make sure that you have data from each stratum (in the right proportions).
  e.g., voting patterns may be different among low, medium and high income groups, so you could sample from each of these strata in the same proportions that they occur in the population as a whole.

- **Cluster sampling**
  This is useful in the opposite situation, when you have different sub-groups of the population that you expect to have *similar* properties. So you just pick one or more of these and choose your sample from among them.
  e.g., milk yields from a particular breed of cows are likely to be similar from similar farms in the same area, so you randomly choose several farms and sample from just them.

- **Quota sampling**
  This involves deciding in advance how many from each strata you want to include in your sample.
  e.g., you ask ten year 10 pupils and ten year 11 pupils what is their favourite subject at school; this method is often used in market research (clipboard people).

- **Systematic sampling**
  This involves choosing every 3rd (or whatever) item from a list. So long as the list is arranged in a random order this will give a random sample.
  e.g., picking every 5th person from a random page of the telephone directory would be a way of systematically sampling people whose names are in the phone book.

3.2 Presenting Data Graphically

- One advantage of frequency polygons over bar charts is that several sets of data can be displayed on the same diagram. (Another solution is to use "compound bar charts", with more than one bar for each category.) One way to illustrate this is to collect some data for boys and for girls separately and then present them on the same graph (see section 3.2.1).

3.2.1 Estimate on scrap paper how long in minutes you spent watching TV last night. If you can't remember, give me your best guess. We're counting between leaving school yesterday and going to bed (not breakfast TV this morning).

Choose sensible groups (e.g., 0-29, 30-59, 60-89 min, etc.).
Tally boys and girls separately and draw two separate diagrams.

Possible hypothesis: "On average, girls watch less TV than boys" (or the opposite).

You can do the same thing with amount of time spent on homework. How does it compare with school expectations?!
Is there any correlation between how much TV pupils watch and how long they spend on their homework? This would require a scatter-graph. (The conclusion is usually that everyone watches far too much TV!)

Some may watch as much as 300 min.

3.2.2 What type of diagram would be suitable for what set of data?

When do we draw pie charts/scatter-graphs, etc.?

What are the advantages/disadvantages of presenting this data in this or that form?

Pupils often find this hard because they are rarely asked such questions.

A pupil may "like" pie charts but not see that they are appropriate only for proportions – when a set of values adds up to a "whole".

This may be an on-going discussion, raised whenever we encounter a new type of diagram/data.

3.2.3 NEED "A Day in the Life" sheets.

A task like this makes drawing pie charts accessible to pupils with no knowledge of angles.

This can make good display work.

Pupils can fill in the data for homework. Bear in mind that it takes from midnight until the next midnight; i.e., two nights!

3.2.4 NEED chocolate wrappers or similar with nutritional information.
Draw a pie chart to illustrate the content of common chocolate bars.

(Note that fat and carbohydrate quantities are often subdivided into saturated/unsaturated and sugars/starch, so you have to be careful not to add these subdivisions to the total and end up with more than 100 g.)

Which bar is "healthiest"?
Is there much difference between them?
How do their prices compare with what's in them?
If you spend more, do you get a healthier product or just a tastier one, or neither?

To make it harder you can assemble a collection of wrappers onto an A4 sheet, removing the "per 100 g" columns so that pupils have to calculate this first.

Multi-pack bags of different items (e.g., chocolate bars) are the best because they often contain full information on the outside of the outer bag for all the items.

Also be careful not to add the amount of energy in kJ or kcal to the mass in grams!

The total normally comes to less than 100 g, so you need to include an "other" sector on the pie chart.

Correlation

Scatter diagrams are a way of comparing two quantities.

- If large values of one tend to go with large values of the other (and small with small) then we have **positive correlation**. The **line of best fit** is the best straight line you can draw through the points. If the points mostly lie close to the line, we say it is *strong* positive correlation. Otherwise it is *weak* positive correlation.

- If large values of one quantity tend to go with small values of the other, then we have **negative correlation**. Depending on how close to the *line of best fit* the points mostly are, we say it is either *strong* or *weak* negative correlation.

- **No correlation** happens when there seems to be no pattern to the arrangement of the points. The two quantities have nothing to do with each other.

positive correlation	strong positive correlation	weak positive correlation	For example, ice-cream sales against temperature
negative correlation	strong negative correlation	weak negative correlation	For example, hot chocolate sales against temperature
no correlation	can't be weak or strong – the points are just scattered randomly (no *line of best fit*)		For example, newspaper sales against temperature

Because two quantities correlate, it doesn't mean that they directly affect one another. It could be that they correlate because they both depend on a third factor that we haven't thought about.

Presenting Data Graphically

- **Bar charts**
  - useful for categorical data (qualitative, non-numerical data)
  - can have horizontal or vertical bars
  - bars don't touch and must have equal width
  - *length* of bars is proportional to the frequency

- **Vertical line graphs**
  - useful for discrete data (data that can take only certain values)
  - vertical axis labelled *frequency*

- **Histograms**
  useful for grouped continuous data (or sometimes grouped discrete data)
  - vertical bars which don't necessarily have equal width
  - bars touch and are labelled on the horizontal axis where they join
  - *area* of bars is proportional to the frequency
  - vertical axis labelled *frequency density* ($= \dfrac{\text{frequency}}{\text{width}}$)

- **Pie charts**
  - area (and angle) of each sector is proportional to the frequency
  - total area is proportional to the total frequency (when comparing different pie charts)

- **Cumulative frequency graphs**
  - useful when you have a total frequency n more than about 30
  - vertical axis is labelled *cumulative frequency*
  - values are plotted against the *upper boundary* of each class
  - points are joined by a smooth curve
  - the **median (Q_2)** is estimated by reading off the $\frac{1}{2}n^{th}$ term
  - the **upper quartile (Q_3)** is estimated from the $\frac{3}{4}n^{th}$ term
  - the **lower quartile (Q_1)** is estimated from the $\frac{1}{4}n^{th}$ term
  - the **inter-quartile range (IQR)** is $Q_3 - Q_1$
    (any data further than 1.5 × IQR beyond the upper or lower quartiles are generally regarded as **outliers**)

- **Median and upper/lower quartiles**
  - For a smaller set of data with n items,
    median $= \frac{1}{2}(n+1)^{th}$ value, and if $\frac{1}{2}(n+1)$ is an integer m then
    upper quartile $= \left[m + \frac{1}{2}(m+1)\right]^{th}$ value and **lower quartile** $= \frac{1}{2}(m+1)^{th}$ value.
    If m is not an integer, round it *down* and then use these formulas.

- **Box and whisker plot (box plot)**
  - useful when drawn underneath the horizontal scale of a cumulative frequency graph or separately with its own scale
  - shows Q_1, Q_2, Q_3 and the maximum and minimum values

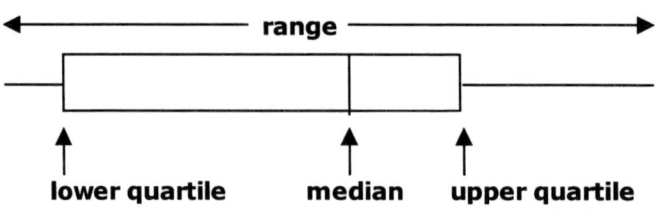

(the labels are not normally needed)

A Day in the Life of _____

time	main activity
0000 – 0100	
0100 – 0200	
0200 – 0300	
0300 – 0400	
0400 – 0500	
0500 – 0600	
0600 – 0700	
0700 - 0800	
0800 – 0900	
0900 – 1000	
1000 – 1100	
1100 – 1200	
1200 – 1300	
1300 – 1400	
1400 – 1500	
1500 – 1600	
1600 – 1700	
1700 – 1800	
1800 – 1900	
1900 – 2000	
2000 – 2100	
2100 – 2200	
2200 – 2300	
2300 – 0000	

In the main activity column, write down the main thing you did during that 1 hour period; e.g., "sleep", "watch TV", "eat lunch", etc.

Then present your activities in the pie chart below. Put the same activity all together, even if you did it at more than one time.

Either write the name of the activity in each sector, or make a key in the space below.

A Pie Chart to Show How I Spent 24 Hours

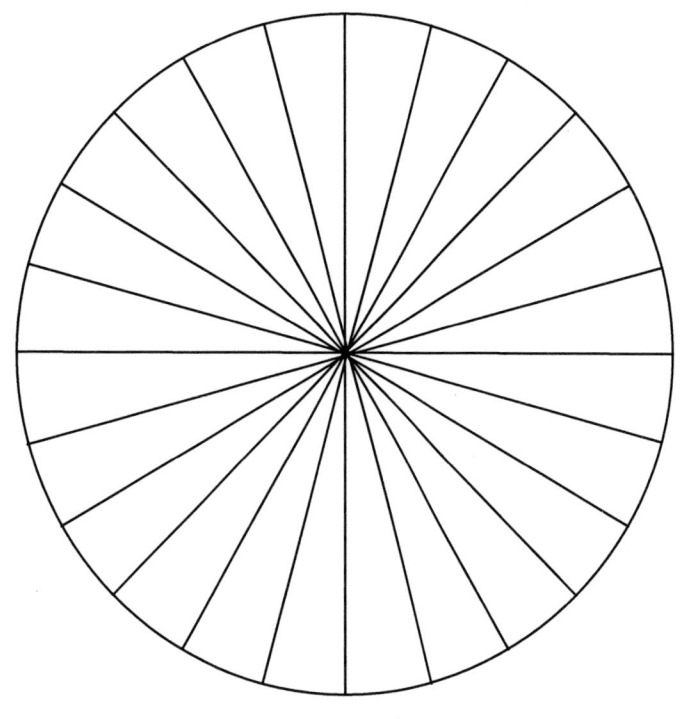

3.3 Statistical Calculations

Mode — The most common value.

Mean — Add up all the values and divide by how many there are.

Median
1. Put all the values in order.
2. Choose the middle value.
3. If there are two middle values (because there are an even number of values) find *their* mean.

Range — The highest value minus the lowest value.

- Here, "mean" always refers to "arithmetic mean".
  "Geometric mean" and "harmonic mean" are much less commonly used.
- To find the median of a large number of values, one way is first to make a stem and leaf diagram. Then the middle value is easily located.
- Pupils should be aware that spreadsheets can easily do these calculations using functions like AVERAGE, MEDIAN, QUARTILE, etc.

3.3.1 Spider diagram of "Descriptive Statistics" (see above). Which one is the odd one out?

Mode is closely linked to probability. If you chose a value at random, the one you'd be most likely to get would be the mode.

It's OK for the mean and median to be "impossible" values (e.g., 2.4 children), but the mode is always an actual value.

Answer:
Range is not a measure of "centre" of the values; it tells you how spread out they are.

If the data are numerical, then there's always a mean and a median, but there isn't necessarily a mode because two or more values may tie for most common, or all the values may be different from each other.
But you can have a mode in some situations where mean and median are impossible; e.g., a modal favourite colour could be "red", but because the data aren't numerical you can't calculate a mean or a median.

3.3.2 Imaginary scores for a game (whatever game you like).
The scores are 3, 1, 5, 0, 1.
What is the "average"?
Is the median 5?

Should we ignore the zero? Will it make any difference to the mean/mode/median/range?

Answers:
mean = 2; median = 1, mode = 1, range = 5
No; you have to put them in order (5 is larger than any of the other values, so it can't be the median).

We can't ignore it if it really happened.
In general it will make a difference. (Imagine that in a maths test one person got 10/10 and everyone else got 0/10. I might like to ignore the 0's, but I can't really!)

3.3.3 Which number is the mean of the other five?

  5 4 5 1 6 3

Answer: 4
Whichever one it is, it doesn't change the mean when it's added in, so the answer will just be the mean of all six values: 24 ÷ 6 = 4.

3.3.4   Mean, Median, Mode, Range (see sheet).

This is more interesting than being given a list of numbers and asked to calculate these quantities.

Pupils can invent similar puzzles.

3.3.5   Possible or Impossible? (see sheet)

This task encourages careful logical thinking and lots of experimentation with finding mean, mode, median and range of invented data.

What if? (see same sheet)

Explores the concept of "linear coding"; the result being that if $y = ax + b$ then $\bar{y} = a\bar{x} + b$. This happens because $\sum y = a\sum x + nb$, so

$$\frac{\sum y}{n} = a\frac{\sum x}{n} + b = a\bar{x} + b.$$

3.3.6   Advantages and Disadvantages (see sheet).
Why do you think we have three different ways of working out an average?
(Is it just to make life complicated?!)

It's important to think through the advantages and disadvantages of each measure and when they are more or less appropriate.

Imagine a company. These are the annual salaries of the people who work there:
£20 000; £20 000; £20 000; £20 000; £20 000; £200 000 (the boss).

What is the mean salary?
The boss writes an advert for a job at his company and he says, "The average salary here is £50 000 per year."
What do you think about that?

Answer: £50 000

It's misleading because everyone except him earns less than half of that! The median and the mode would be more honest here.

Think of a situation where the mode or the median would be misleading.

The boss might say to the shareholders, "Our average (median/mode) salary for the whole staff is only £20 000". This conceals his "fat-cat" salary!

It can be fun to invent similar scenarios.

3.3.7   "Birthdays are good for you. Statistics show that people who have the most birthdays live the longest!"
Why is that silly?

Answer: birthdays just measure how many years you've been alive – correlation doesn't mean that one thing causes the other to happen.

3.3.8   **NEED** "Routes to School" sheets (2 copies on the sheet).

Answers:

route	mean	mode	median	range
A	21.95	22	22	16
B	21.6	24	21	11

Maths tells you the likelihood of being on time if you travel by different routes, but it can't tell you what you should do – something may be more important to you than arriving as quickly as possible; e.g., travelling with a particular friend.

Pupils could mention other relevant factors, such as preferring to walk or take the bus, perhaps differently depending on the weather.

Pupils could write their answers "to James", offering him mathematical advice.

3.3.9   Discussion: "You can prove anything with statistics." Do you agree or disagree?

It was probably Disraeli (1804-1881) who said that there are "lies, damned lies and statistics".

Perhaps the answer is that statistics can be and are misused. All the more reason for understanding the subject so that the wool won't be pulled over your eyes!

Instant Maths Ideas: 3

Mean, Median, Mode, Range

In all these questions only use numbers which are *positive integers* (or zero).

1   Find five numbers with a mean of 10.

    How many possibilities can you find?

2   Find five numbers with a mean of 10 and with a median that isn't 10.

3   Find five numbers with a mean of 10 and no mode.

4   Find five numbers with a mean of 10, a median of 7 and a mode of 7.
    (Hint: start with 7 in the middle)

5   Find five numbers with a mean of 4, a mode of 5, a median of 5 and a range of 5.

6   Find five numbers with a mean of 6, a mode of 8, a median of 6 and a range of 5.

7   Find five numbers with a mean of 9, a mode of 7, a median of 8 and a range of 7.

Challenge

Can you find four positive integers such that mean < mode < median?
Explain your answer.

What if they don't have to be positive integers?

What other statistical inequalities can you make definite statements about?

Mean, Median, Mode, Range

In all these questions only use numbers which are positive integers (or zero).

1. Find five numbers with a mean of 10. How many possibilities can you find?

    Any set of 5 numbers that sum to 50 will do, because when you divide by 5 you'll get 10.

e.g.	8	9	10	11	12
	10	10	10	10	10
	6	8	10	12	14
	0	0	0	0	50
	0	5	10	15	20

2. Find five numbers with a mean of 10 and with a median that isn't 10.

e.g.	0	0	0	0	50
	0	1	2	22	25

3. Find five numbers with a mean of 10 and no mode.

e.g.	8	9	10	11	12
	0	1	2	22	25

4. Find five numbers with a mean of 10, a median of 7 and a mode of 7.
   (Hint: start with 7 in the middle)

e.g.	6	7	7	12	18
	7	7	7	7	22

5. Find five numbers with a mean of 4, a mode of 5, a median of 5 and a range of 5.

e.g.	1	3	5	5	6

6. Find five numbers with a mean of 6, a mode of 8, a median of 6 and a range of 5.

e.g.	3	5	6	8	8

7. Find five numbers with a mean of 9, a mode of 7, a median of 8 and a range of 7.

e.g.	7	7	8	9	1

Challenge

Can you find four positive integers such that mean < mode < median? Explain your answer.
What if they don't have to be positive integers?

Let the four numbers in order from smallest to largest be a, b, c, d (so $a \leq b \leq c \leq d$).
If there is a mode, then two, three or all four must be equal. (If two are equal, then the other two mustn't be equal to each other – unless all four are equal.)
If all four are equal, then the inequality cannot hold because all three averages would equal the same amount.
If three are equal, then $b = c$ necessarily, so median = mode, contradicting the inequality.
So if it's possible at all, it must be when two of the values (but not b and c) are equal.
If $c = d \neq b$, then mode > median.
So the only possibility is $a = b$, (and mode < median), but then the mean $= \frac{1}{4}(a+a+c+d)$ which must be >
a, so mean > mode, contradicting the inequality. So, impossible, even without the restriction that the numbers have to be positive integers.

Instant Maths Ideas: 3

Possible or Impossible?

I have a set of numerical values which could be anything, and I want to know whether each of these statements (separately) is possible or impossible.

Can it apply to the *mean*, the *median*, the *mode* or the *range*?

If it's possible, give an example; if impossible, try to say why.

statement	mean	median	mode	range
There isn't one.				
It's equal to zero.				
It's the highest value.				
It's the lowest value.				
It's greater than any of the values.				
It's less than any of the values.				

What if ...?

You have a set of values and you've worked out the mean.

What will happen to the mean if ...

1   you add 10 to all the values?
2   you subtract 10 from all the values?
3   you multiply all the values by 10?
4   you divide all the values by 10?
5   you square all the values?

Make up some numbers and try it.
Try to explain your answers.

Possible or Impossible?

I have a set of numerical values which could be anything, and I want to know whether each of these statements (separately) is possible or impossible.
Can it apply to the *mean*, the *median*, the *mode* or the *range*?
If it's possible, give an example; if impossible, try to say why.

statement	mean	median	mode	range
There isn't one.	Impossible, provided all the values are numbers.	Impossible, provided all the values are numbers.	Possible; e.g., 1, 2, 3, 4, 5.	Impossible, provided all the values are numbers.
It's equal to zero.	Possible if all the values are zero or some are negative so that their total comes to zero.	Possible if all the values are zero or some are negative so that the median happens to be zero.	Possible; e.g., 0, 0, 1, 2, 3.	Possible if all the values are equal; e.g., 5, 5, 5, 5, 5.
It's the highest value.	Possible only if all the values are the same.	Possible only if all the values are the same.	Possible; e.g., 1, 2, 3, 4, 4.	Possible if the lowest value is zero.
It's the lowest value.	Possible only if all the values are the same.	Possible only if all the values are the same.	Possible; e.g., 1, 1, 2, 3, 4.	Possible if the highest value is twice the lowest value; e.g., 3, 4, 5, 6.
It's greater than any of the values.	Impossible, because the mean represents equal shares of the total amount.	Impossible, because the "middle" value can't be more than any of them.	Impossible, because it must be an actual value.	Possible if the lowest value is negative; e.g., –2, 3, 4, 5.
It's less than any of the values.	Impossible, because the mean represents equal shares of the total amount.	Impossible, because the "middle" value can't be less than any of them.	Impossible, because it must be an actual value.	Possible if the values are not very spread out compared with their size; e.g., 7, 8, 9, 10.

What if ...?

You have a set of values and you've worked out the mean.
What will happen to the mean if ...

1. you add 10 to all the values? *mean goes up by 10*
2. you subtract 10 from all the values? *mean goes down by 10*
3. you multiply all the values by 10? *mean is multiplied by 10*
4. you divide all the values by 10? *mean is divided by 10*
5. you square all the values? *no simple answer;*

$$\frac{\sum x^2}{n} \neq \left(\frac{\sum x}{n}\right)^2,$$ *so the answer is* **not** *the square of the mean.*

Make up some numbers and try it. Try to explain your answers.

Advantages and Disadvantages

What are some of the advantages and disadvantages of using the mean, the mode and the median as averages representing the whole set of data?

	advantages	disadvantages
mean	• takes all the data into account; • well-known and understood ("equal shares");	• swayed by extreme values; • works only with numbers (e.g., not with colours); • not always a possible value (e.g., "2.4 children"); • sometimes it's too much work to do the calculation;
median	• not affected by extreme values; • can be approximated from cumulative frequency curves; • often a possible value (e.g., it's often an integer if the data have to be integers);	• ignores the actual values of most of the data; • works only with numbers that can be ordered (e.g., not with colours); • sometimes it's inconvenient to have to put all the data in order first;
mode	• not affected by one extreme value; • works with qualitative data (e.g., colours) as well as with numbers; • always a possible value (e.g., an integer if the data have to be integers); • useful in probability work;	• ignores the actual values of much of the data; • there isn't always a mode;

Make up an example to illustrate each of the points above.

What other advantages and disadvantages can you think of?

Routes to School

James has two possible ways of getting to school:

A   He can catch a bus into the town centre and another bus out; or
B   He can walk in a different direction and then just catch one (different) bus.

He isn't sure which way is quicker so he decides to time his journey from leaving his front door to arriving at the school gate. He times 20 journeys by route **A** and 20 by route **B**.
Here are his results (in minutes).

Route A
24	18	14	19	22	23	18	15	22	30
30	26	22	27	16	22	26	19	19	27

Route B
25	18	21	18	28	21	17	19	26	24
25	24	21	17	20	22	24	20	24	18

Work out the mean, median, mode and range for the times for route **A** and for route **B**.
Which route do you think James should use, and why?

Routes to School

James has two possible ways of getting to school:

A   He can catch a bus into the town centre and another bus out; or
B   He can walk in a different direction and then just catch one (different) bus.

He isn't sure which way is quicker so he decides to time his journey from leaving his front door to arriving at the school gate. He times 20 journeys by route **A** and 20 by route **B**.
Here are his results (in minutes).

Route A
24	18	14	19	22	23	18	15	22	30
30	26	22	27	16	22	26	19	19	27

Route B
25	18	21	18	28	21	17	19	26	24
25	24	21	17	20	22	24	20	24	18

Work out the mean, median, mode and range for the times for route **A** and for route **B**.
Which route do you think James should use, and why?

Statistical Calculations

- **Discrete** data – only certain values are possible (e.g., shoe sizes: 1, 1.5, 2, etc.).
- **Continuous** data – any value is possible within a certain range (e.g., heights of pupils measured in cm).
- **Stem and leaf diagrams** – remember to include a **key** and to use LOW and HIGH for extreme values that are hard to fit on the scale. If there's a lot of data on each line you can do a **stretched** version with, say, 0-4 on one line and 5-9 on the next.
  Good for finding the median and seeing the general shape.
- **Mean** (arithmetic mean): add up all the values and divide by how many there are.
  $$\bar{x} = \frac{\sum x}{n}$$
  This shares out the total x evenly, but it can be distorted by exceptionally large or small values, and the answer may not be a possible actual value (e.g., "2.4 children").
  For data where there are f occurrences of each x, we use the formula
  $$\bar{x} = \frac{\sum fx}{\sum f}$$
  For grouped data, x has to be the mid-point of the class.
- **Mode** (or **modal class** for grouped data): most frequent value.
  Often easy to find, but there isn't always one.
  There may be just one mode (**unimodal**) or there may be two values – not necessarily equally frequent – that are more common than the rest (**bimodal**).
  Useful if you want the most probable value or if you're using qualitative data (e.g., modal favourite colour – you can't work out a "mean colour").
  Data may be **skewed positively** (mode to the left, long tail to the right) or **negatively** (the opposite).
- **Median**: the middle value when they're listed in order (or the mean of the two middle values where there are an even number of data).
  Often easy to find, especially from a stem and leaf diagram.
  Not affected by extreme or missing values.
- **Mid-range**: the mean of the highest and lowest values.
  Good for fairly symmetrical data but dependent on the most extreme values.
- **Range**: the highest value minus the lowest.
  Easy to calculate but dependent on the most extreme values.
- **Mean absolute deviation from the mean**: $\dfrac{\sum f|x-\bar{x}|}{\sum f}$.
- **Variance**: defined as the mean of the square deviations from the mean: $\dfrac{\sum f(x-\bar{x})^2}{\sum f}$, but for calculations it's easier to use $\dfrac{\sum x^2}{n} - \bar{x}^2$, or for data where there are f occurrences of each x we use the formula $\dfrac{\sum fx^2}{\sum f} - \bar{x}^2$.
- **Standard deviation**: the positive square root of the variance. Data which are more than two standard deviations above or below the mean are exceptional and may be classed as **outliers**. There may be a special reason for these values.
- **Linear coding**: Imagine you have a set of data (x) with mean $\bar{x}$ and standard deviation $\text{sd}(x)$. If you modify each value so that you create a new variable y so that $y = ax + b$, then that will affect the mean and standard deviation so that the new mean $\bar{y}$ and new standard deviation $\text{sd}(y)$ will be $\bar{y} = a\bar{x} + b$ and $\text{sd}(y) = a \times \text{sd}(x)$.

3.4 Combinations

- "Combinations" refers to the number of ways that things can happen or be done.
  "Permutations" includes all the different orders that those combinations could come in.
- "Pascal's Triangle" is sometimes called the "Chinese Triangle", because it pre-dates Blaise Pascal (1623-1662) by hundreds of years.

•3.4.1 Braille.
Braille is an arrangement of between 0 and 6 raised dots in a 2 × 3 rectangle;
e.g., the letter E is

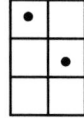

(the lines of the rectangle are not normally drawn in).

How many other possible arrangements can you make just using 2 dots?
How many arrangements can you make if you can use any number of dots from 0 to 6.

(Every square can be either a "dot" or "no-dot" – that explains why $d = 2$ and $d = 5$ have the same number of arrangements – their arrangements are like "negatives" of each other.)

Are there enough different arrangements to cover the alphabet, digits and necessary symbols like full stop?

It would be good to have some Braille books to look at and to try to decipher (using a Braille alphabet – available, for example, on the internet).

3.4.2 Investigating Pascal's Triangle.
Write out Pascal's Triangle as far as the 7th or 8th row at least (see sheet).

Look for these types of numbers and describe where they come in the triangle.

1. lines of "1"'s;
2. natural numbers;
3. triangle numbers;
4. tetrahedron numbers;
5. powers of 2;
6. powers of 11;
7. ^nC_r

What other patterns can you find?

(See the sheet for further details.)

Answers:

number of dots	number of arrangements
0	1
1	6
2	15
3	20
4	15
5	6
6	1

If the number of dots is d, then the number of arrangements is ^6C_d. These numbers are the seventh line of Pascal's triangle.

$$^6C_d = \frac{6!}{(6-d)!d!}$$

The total number of arrangements is $2^6 = 64$, because there are two possibilities for each square and there are six squares.

This is plenty of characters.

Answers:
1. *diagonally down each side;*
2. *diagonal lines next to the diagonals of 1's;*
3. *the next diagonal lines to the natural numbers;*
4. *the next diagonal lines to the triangle numbers;*
5. *the sums of each horizontal row;*
6. *the digits along each row up to and including the 5th row;*
7. *the $(r+1)^{th}$ number (or the $(n-r)^{th}$ number) along in the $(n+1)^{th}$ row.*

If you shade in the squares containing odd numbers and leave the other squares white, you get the so-called Sierpinski Triangle (1882-1969). This drawing is a fractal (when you zoom out it looks the same).

Instant Maths Ideas: 3

3.4.3 Why must there be at least two people in the world with the same number of hairs on their heads?

It's obvious that if you have two completely bald people, then they have the same number (0) of hairs on their heads.

Answer: There are more people in the world than there are hairs on anyone's head, so everyone can't have a different number of hairs (pigeonhole principle)!

Some pupils may question this assumption, but 6.5×10^9 hairs would be a very hairy person!

3.4.4 **NEED** Squared paper, preferably at least as big as a 2 cm × 2 cm squared grid (see sheet).
Routes through a Grid.
If you're going from one place to somewhere else in a city, then there may be more than one way of getting there.
Generally, that's complicated, but it's simpler in New York (or Milton Keynes) because of the way the streets are laid out.

Does anyone know what's special about the layout of the streets in New York?

Roads are laid out so that they mostly cross one another at 90° (see right). North-South roads are called avenues, *and East-West roads are called* streets. *They're numbered from 1st (south-east corner). (So a junction can be described as "5th avenue, 42nd street", for instance.)*

Investigate routes through a simplified version. Write on the diagram the number of ways of getting from the start (top left corner) to each crossroads.
You are only allowed to go right and down, because we want routes that are as short as possible (never go back towards the start).

Can you explain your results?

Once you see what is going on, try to complete the pattern of numbers.

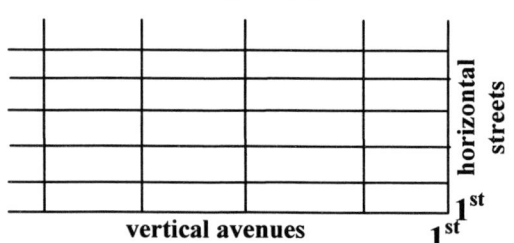

The avenues are split into "short blocks" (about $\frac{1}{20}$ mile); the streets into "long blocks" (about $\frac{1}{4}$ mile). Milton Keynes uses a system based on H (horizontal) and V (vertical).

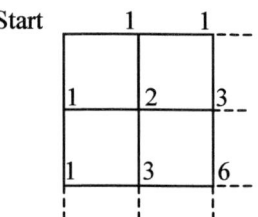

Pascal's triangle. (We have to say that there is "1 way" of getting to the "start".)

Wherever you are you must have come via the position immediately above or the position immediately to the left. So the number of ways of reaching any position is the sum of the numbers of ways of reaching these two positions. That generates Pascal's Triangle.

3.4.5 I write 6 letters and address 6 envelopes. I put each letter into an envelope. How many ways are there of getting every letter in the *wrong* envelope?

This is called the number of "derangements".
It turns out that $!n = \left[\dfrac{n!}{e}\right]$, where the square brackets indicate that you round the answer to the nearest integer.

Answer: Very hard!
$$6!\left(\frac{1}{2!} - \frac{1}{3!} + \frac{1}{4!} - \frac{1}{5!} + \frac{1}{6!}\right) = 265 \text{ ways}$$
This is called "6 sub-factorial" and written !6 (instead of 6!).

In general, $!n = n!\sum_{i=0}^{n}\dfrac{(-1)^i}{i!}$

3.4.6 How many ways are there of arranging the letters in your name. (The rearrangements don't have to make real words!)
e.g., for GEORGE it is $\frac{6!}{2!2!} = 180$ *(because of the two G's and two E's).*

Answer: If the name contains a letters, of which b are the same as each other, c are the same as each other, etc., then the number of arrangements is $\dfrac{a!}{b!c!...}$.

3.4.7 Find out what "entropy" is and why it is important in Science.

This is called the "2nd Law of Thermodynamics".

Answer: Entropy is a measure of how "disordered" a system is; the total entropy of the universe always increases when anything happens.

Pascal's Triangle and ^nC_r Values

r value

		0	1	2	3	4	5	6	7	8	9	10
n value	0	1										
	1	1	1									
	2	1	2	1								
	3	1	3	3	1							
	4	1	4	6	4	1						
	5	1	5	10	10	5	1					
	6	1	6	15	20	15	6	1				
	7	1	7	21	35	35	21	7	1			
	8	1	8	28	56	70	56	28	8	1		
	9	1	9	36	84	126	126	84	36	9	1	
	10	1	10	45	120	210	252	210	120	45	10	1

^nC_r is the number of ways (regardless of the order) of choosing *r* things from *n* things.

$$^nC_r = \frac{n!}{(n-r)!r!} \text{ and } 0! = 1$$

- $^nC_0$ and ^nC_n are always 1 (there's one way of choosing no objects, and one way of choosing the whole lot).
- ^nC_r and $^nC_{n-r}$ are always the same as each other (if you choose *r* objects, you've inevitably chosen (*n* – *r*) objects, because they're the ones you've left behind).
- $^nC_1$ and $^nC_{n-1}$ are always *n* (there are *n* ways of choosing just 1 [it could be any of them] and *n* ways of leaving just 1 behind [again, it could be any of them]).
- From the table above, you can see that $^{n-1}C_{r-1} + {}^{n-1}C_r = {}^nC_r$, and

$$\frac{(n-1)!}{(n-1-(r-1))!(r-1)!} + \frac{(n-1)!}{(n-1-r)!r!}$$

$$= \frac{(n-1)!r}{(n-r)!r!} + \frac{(n-1)!(n-r)}{(n-r)!r!}$$

$$= \frac{(n-1)!(r+(n-r))}{(n-r)!r!} = \frac{(n-1)!n}{(n-r)!r!} = \frac{n!}{(n-r)!r!}$$

To understand this, think about 1 of the *n* objects separately from the other (*n* – *1*) objects.
This one is either included in your choice of objects or it isn't.
If it is, then there are (*r* – *1*) objects left to choose from (*n* – 1) [$^{n-1}C_{r-1}$ ways of doing that].
On the other hand, if that object *isn't* included, then you have to choose all *r* objects from only (*n* – 1) objects, and there are $^{n-1}C_r$ ways of doing that.
These two possibilities we've been thinking about are *mutually exclusive*, so the total number of ways of choosing *r* objects from *n* will be the sum of these two numbers;
i.e., $^{n-1}C_{r-1} + {}^{n-1}C_r = {}^nC_r$.
If you can follow this, you're doing well!

Start

Start

3.5 Probability

- A topic where there are many misconceptions, partly due to problems with ratio thinking, partly due to not recognising the assumptions behind the theory. A crucial concept is the one of "equally likely outcomes". Pupils can mindlessly put one number over another number to create fractions that represent probabilities without any understanding of the size of these values. For this reason it can be an advantage to use decimals some of the time in early probability work.
- You could allow pupils to leave fractions unsimplified if that is a major hurdle in this topic.
- Sample space diagrams are generally easier to draw and use than tree diagrams, but are limited to situations where there are two events.
- For three or more events, tree diagrams are needed. Some "blanks" are given on sheets for those pupils who find it hard to judge the layout: when drawing tree diagrams, it can sometimes be easiest to start at the right side (where there are lots of branches) and work your way to the left.
- You may need to teach the composition of a standard pack of cards:
  Excluding jokers, there are 52 cards made up of 4 suits (hearts, diamonds, spades and clubs) each containing 13 cards (ace, 2, 3, 4, 5, 6, 7, 8, 9, 10, jack, queen, king). Hearts and diamonds are red; spades and clubs black. Ace may be "high" or "low". Jack, queen, king count as "picture cards". (Some pupils/parents may object to gambling contexts or any use of playing cards.)
- For practical work, throwing dice is much quieter if they're thrown onto a book or into a small cardboard box rather than onto a desk! – a box also makes them less likely to fall on the floor.
- Dictionaries now seem to allow *dice* (as well as *die*) as the singular.

3.5.1 Probability Scales.
Everybody talks about probability using words such as "likely", "even chance", "almost certain", etc. Mathematicians simply make it more precise by using a scale of numbers.
Numbers between 0 and 1 can be fractions, decimals or percentages.

It's like the difference between describing temperature as "fairly hot" and using the Celsius temperature scale.
(Except that the probability scale has ends at 0 and 1. The temperature scale has an end at absolute zero, –273 °C, but no clear cut-off at the upper end.)

3.5.2 NEED carrier bag and coloured cubes.
A useful way of discussing simple probability.
If I want a probability of 0.5 (even chance) of pulling out a red cube, what could I put in?, etc.

You need to use a thick or dark-coloured carrier bag so that you can't see the cubes inside. (Cloth money bags, available from banks, are ideal for this.)

3.5.3 Imagine I have 12 red cubes and 4 blue cubes in a bag. So $p(\text{red}) = 0.75$ and $p(\text{blue}) = 0.25$.
Imagine I will give you 20 pence if you correctly guess the colour of the cube I pull out at random.
Imagine we play this game again and again. What would you guess?

Answer:
The best strategy is to guess red every time, because if the draws are truly random then every go is more likely to turn out red than blue.
Some pupils will feel that you ought to guess blue a quarter of the time, but the problem is that we don't know which quarter of the goes will be blue! This gets us to the idea of "independent" events.

How much would be a fair amount to charge people to play this game?

Clearly 20p or more would be too much (no-one would play!). On average, if people guess "red" every time, they will win $0.75 \times 20 = 15$ p per go, so in the long run charging 15 p you would break even. Perhaps you would charge 15 p and hope that people will not always choose red, and so on average you should make a profit.

3.5.4 NEED "Number Probabilities" sheet.

This is an opportunity to review words and concepts like multiple, factor, prime, square, triangle, power, etc.

Answers:
1. $\frac{1}{10}$; 2. $\frac{1}{5}$; 3. $\frac{1}{2}$; 4. $\frac{1}{10}$; 5. $\frac{1}{25}$; 6. $\frac{19}{20}$; 7. $\frac{1}{11}$;
8. $\frac{9}{10}$; 9. $\frac{1}{100}$; 10. $\frac{3}{50}$ (remembering that 1 is a factor of every number); 11. $\frac{2}{25}$; 12. $\frac{1}{50}$; 13. $\frac{9}{100}$;

Instant Maths Ideas: 3

If you can afford to use the sheets only once, pupils may prefer to colour in the appropriate numbers in the number square for each question as they go.
Or you could use the 100-squares given in section 1.16.

3.5.5 Invent a Fair Game.
What about this one – is it fair?
Who's likely to do better out of it in the long run?

"You pay me £1 to play. You throw two fair dice and if you get a double I give you £5. Otherwise you lose your money."

Can you alter this game to make it fair?

We could add this rule: "If you get a total score of 7, I have to give you your money back."
Since there is a $\frac{1}{6}$ chance of this happening, overall neither of us would make or lose money playing the game.

3.5.6 **NEED** dice. Two Dice Experiment.
A fun way to do this is to have a "horse race".
On scrap paper, draw out a table as on the right (or use the sheet).

The 12 rows represent the tracks for 12 horses. Choose a horse to "bet" on (no money!).
Then throw two dice, add up the scores and that horse moves on one place.
Keep going until a horse reaches the finishing line. That one's the winner.

This works best in pairs. Each person bets on a different horse. One person throws the dice and the other marks with an X the current positions of the horses.

After seeing what happens, try to make a more successful bet on your second go.

Is this a fair game? Are some horses more likely to win? Why is that?

14. $\frac{1}{10}$ *(remembering that 1 is the first square number)*; 15. $\frac{1}{2}$; 16. $\frac{7}{100}$; 17. $\frac{3}{50}$ *(or $\frac{7}{100}$ if you count $2^0 = 1$)*; 18. $\frac{33}{100}$ *(not $\frac{1}{3}$)*; 19. $\frac{13}{100}$; 20. $\frac{1}{4}$ *(remembering that 1 doesn't count as a prime number)*.

Pupils need to be encouraged to keep it very simple. Even relatively simple games can be highly challenging to analyse!

Not fair on you, because p(double) = $\frac{1}{6}$, so

	your gain per go
1. You pay me £1.	−1
2. Throw the dice	$+5 \times \frac{1}{6}$
total	$-1 + \frac{5}{6} = -\frac{1}{6}$

So on average I will gain £1 of yours every 6 goes.

These games seem pretty pointless, since there is no element of skill, but games of chance are popular, perhaps partly because people don't understand probability! However, some people enjoy the game even though they don't expect to win anything playing.

Many pupils are shocked to discover that the scores with two dice aren't all equally likely.

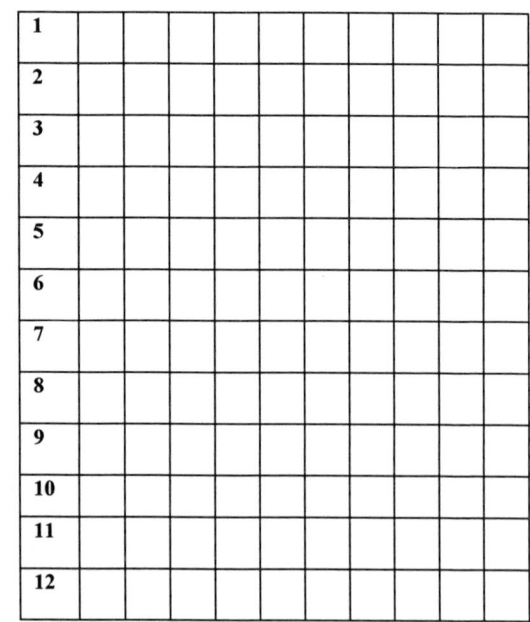

(ten columns after the column of numbers)

Some pupils may realise quickly that horse 1 is a no-hoper!

Sample Space diagrams are the ideal way to explain the results.

3.5.7 **NEED** "Statements About Probability" sheets.
One way to use these is to cut them into 10 separate statements and distribute them to different people. Then hold a discussion in which one by one people read out their statements and they or others comment on them.
"Do you understand what they're meaning?"
"Why would someone think that?"
"Do you agree?"
"Can you explain why in your own words?"
"Can you think of another example of that?"

Alternatively, pupils can discuss the statements in small groups.

Many pupils will be quite happy with the statements as they are, so this is a good way to tackle misconceptions.
You may not manage to convince everybody about everything in this one task!

If the probability of the birth of a boy is greater than the probability of the birth of a girl, why isn't the world over-populated with men?
A complicated issue, but part of the answer is that baby girls are slightly more likely to survive into adulthood.

Answers:
1. *Not true. They're not equally likely events; e.g., consider snow/not, earthquake/not, winning/not winning the National Lottery!*
2. *Not true. Proportionate thinking is necessary, and the probability of getting red from bag A ($\frac{2}{3}$) is actually greater than from bag B ($\frac{10}{17}$).*
3. *The coin is likely to be biased, but it's theoretically possible for an unbiased coin to do this.*
4. *Not true. The probability is $\left(\frac{1}{2}\right)^{50}$ in both cases, because each throw is an inde-pendent event: the coin has no memory!*
5. *If the outcome is affected by skill or "luck" then the probability is not exactly $\frac{1}{6}$. This value refers to a random process.*
6. *Similar to 5. Selecting different cards are not equally likely outcomes for this person.*
7. *Similar to 4. Not true. The probability is $\left(\frac{1}{6}\right)^2$ in both cases, because each dice is unaffected by the other: independent events.*
8. *Not true. Two consecutive tickets are no less likely than any other pair. If the draw is fair, every ticket is equally likely to be picked. So are every pair of tickets.*
9. *You could argue about the biology, but births are probably independent events, and the probability of a baby boy is about $\frac{1}{2}$ (but in fact just slightly greater). This misconception is often called the "Gambler's Fallacy".*
10. *Although it's silly, it can be a tricky one to explain. Whether someone else decides to bring a bomb is not affected by whether I do, because they're independent events.*

3.5.8 If you throw two ordinary dice, you can get any number from 2 to 12, but they're not all equally likely. By changing the numbers on the faces of the dice (say, using stickers), can you create two dice so that every score from 2 to 12 is equally likely?

You could use 33 of the 36 combinations but it's harder to make a close link between the numbers on the dice and what you need to count as the score.

Can you do it if you want every total from 1 to 12 to be equally likely?

Yes, but not simply – you have to "waste" some throws. One method would be to say that you will throw again if you get (2,3), (2,4), (2,5), (3,2), (3,3), (3,4), (3,5), (4,2), (4,3), (4,4), (4,5), (5,2), (5,3) or (5,5). This leaves 22 possible combinations (which is divisible by 11), so now we can count the total score on the dice, except that (2,2) has to count as 2 (not 4) and (5,5) has to count as 12 (not 10). So long as you remember that, it isn't too bad, but it's pretty complicated.

Yes (much easier); e.g., change one dice so that three faces show a 0 and the other three a 6.

3.5.9 If you wanted a series of random numbers between 1 and 5, what kind of dice would you need?

What if you wanted random numbers between 1 and 8?

A normal 6-sided dice would do, if you just ignore the throw every time you get a 6 (or stick a piece of paper over the 6 – although that might affect how the dice lands).

You'd need a dice with more faces or a more complicated system.

Instant Maths Ideas: 3

3.5.10 Three Dice Experiment.
Choose a number between 1 and 20 – you can't change it once you've chosen.
Throw three dice 20 times and do a tally of the total scores.
Which score comes up most often?
Change your target number. What is the best target number?

Can we explain the results?
How can you get a total of 5, say?

Divide the possible totals among the class so that in groups pupils work out the number of ways of getting each total.

Pool the results and put them into a table (see sheet).

This is an interesting, and much harder, variation for pupils who are already familiar with the "Two Dice Experiment".

(1, 2, 19 and 20 are impossible scores.)

*In fact, the most probable score is 10 or 11.
You can pool results from the whole class.*

1, 1, 3 (3 ways) or 1, 2, 2 (3 ways), so 6 ways in total. (You can imagine that the three dice are red, blue and green if that helps to see the number of permutations of each combination.)

(There is one way of arranging AAA, 3 ways of arranging AAB and 6 ways of arranging ABC.)

3.5.11 Buffon's Needle (Comte de Buffon, 1707-1788).
This 18th century problem asks what the probability is of dropping a needle onto a set of parallel lines and it landing *across* one of the lines. The length of the needle is the same as the spacing between the lines.

If the spacing x between the lines is larger than the needle length l, the probability of a hit becomes $\frac{2l}{\pi x}$.

*Answer:
If the length of the needle is 1 unit and it falls at an angle θ to the lines, then it will cross the lines if its centre is closer than $\frac{1}{2}\sin\theta$ to the lines, and the locus of these points makes up a fraction $\sin\theta$ of the whole area, so the probability of a hit =*

$$\frac{1}{\left(\frac{\pi}{2}\right)}\int_0^{\frac{\pi}{2}} \sin\theta\, d\theta = \frac{2}{\pi}.$$

*In principle you could use this method to estimate the value of π, but in practice it is a lot of work to get a reasonable degree of accuracy.
Computer simulations of the experiment do give an accurate value for lots of throws.*

3.5.12 Paving Slabs (the Buffon-Laplace Needle Problem).
NEED 2.5 cm long sticks and 5 cm × 5 cm squared paper (see sheet).

Pupils drop the stick onto the sheet of squares and record a "hit" if any part of the stick lies over any line, and a "miss" otherwise.

You can repeat the experiment (or different groups of pupils can try it) using shorter (1 cm) sticks.

In general, if l is the stick length and the grid rectangles are x by y ($l < x$ and $l < y$), then the probability of a hit is given by $\frac{2l(x+y)-l^2}{\pi xy}$. If we let $y \to \infty$, this probability becomes $\frac{2l}{\pi x}$, the result for parallel lines.

This is an alternative, based on Buffon's Needle (above), to the classic experiment where pupils drop a drawing pin and record whether it lands point up or point down.

You can plot a graph of "relative frequency so far" against the number of throws. This usually shows that the relative frequency settles down to a steady value – this value would be our estimate for the probability of a hit.

Using trigonometry and calculus, the theoretical probability of a hit is $\frac{7}{4\pi} = 0.56$ (2 dp).

With a 1 cm long stick (probably the smallest practicable length), the theoretical probability of a hit is $\frac{19}{25\pi} = 0.24$ (2 dp).

3.5.13 Working Out Probabilities (see sheet).

It's helpful to be explicit about the different methods we use to arrive at probabilities. Some pupils will think that "calculating is good and experimenting is bad".

3.5.14 Is *anything* absolutely impossible ($p = 0$) or completely certain ($p = 1$)?

Logically, if you are certain that something is impossible, then you have a complete certainty and an absolute impossibility, so you've killed two birds with one stone!

Answer:
This is really a philosophical question. Jokes aside (e.g., the probability of a certain football team ever winning a match, etc.), you could say that some things are intrinsically impossible; e.g., the probability of finding a triangle with four sides or discovering that $2 + 2 = 5$.
Other non-mathematical contradictory events could be "me being at school and not being at school at the same time", etc.
As for complete certainty, some may argue that we may be completely sure about some religious statements because God is completely trustworthy.

3.5.15 How many people must you have together in a room before there is a greater than 50% chance of at least two of them having the same birthday?

(We ignore birthdays on 29 February here.)

If there were more than 365 people, you wouldn't need to do any calculations, because the pigeonhole principle would say that there must be at least two people with the same birthday. (You can't share around 365 different birthdays among more than 365 people.)

Answer:
23 people, because p(everyone has a different birthday) = $\dfrac{^{365}C_{23}}{365^{23}} = 0.493$ (3 dp), since there are only 365 different birthdays available. Since this is less than 0.5, and if you work it out for 22 people it's just greater than 0.5, then 23 is the minimum number of people.

If you tried the above approach with more than 365, you would be trying to calculate $^{365}C_r$ where $r > 365$, and that is meaningless.

3.5.16 Find out what the "Monty Hall Problem" is – or tell them …

It's a famous conundrum. Imagine I have three identical-looking boxes, one of which contains a chocolate bar. I know which box the chocolate is in, but you don't.
You have to choose a box. Then I will open one of the *other two* boxes, but I will always open one with nothing in it. (I can always do that because there are three boxes, and even if you choose an empty one there will always be another empty one I can open.)
Now you can choose to stick with the box you've got or to swap to the other unopened box. The question is what is the best thing to do? Should you stay or swap?

In fact you're better off swapping. The easiest way to see this (and it's still not that easy to see!) is to imagine a hundred boxes instead of just three. After you've chosen a box, I open all the others except one (and except yours) and they're all empty. It's highly likely that the only reason I didn't open yours is that you'd chosen it. The chocolate is almost certainly in the other box that I declined to open. So swapping is definitely better.

An enjoyable discussion. If no-one has anything to say, give pupils time to discuss in pairs/groups before presenting their ideas to the whole class.

(Obviously, this assumes that you like chocolate and want to win the bar!)

This can lead to lively debate. It works well if the teacher is devil's advocate.
If they say "swap", you could ask "Has opening the third box really told you anything about the two unopened boxes?"
If they say "stay", you could ask "You picked it out of three possibles; now there are only two possibles isn't it more likely to be the other one?"

Another way to see it is like this: Call the boxes A, B and C. Imagine that the prize is in box A, but of course you don't know that. You must start by choosing A, B or C at random.
If you choose A, I can open B or C, but either way you lose if you swap.
If you choose B, I will have to open C and you will win if you swap.
If you choose C, I will have to open B and you will win if you swap.
So $\frac{2}{3}$ of the time, swapping is better.

3.5.17 A stick is broken into 3 pieces. What is the probability that they will make a triangle?

Answer: It turns out to be $\frac{1}{4}$. You can prove it by thinking about 4 congruent equilateral triangles with sides equal to the length of the stick.

Number Probabilities

1	2	3	4	5	6	7	8	9	10
11	12	13	14	15	16	17	18	19	20
21	22	23	24	25	26	27	28	29	30
31	32	33	34	35	36	37	38	39	40
41	42	43	44	45	46	47	48	49	50
51	52	53	54	55	56	57	58	59	60
61	62	63	64	65	66	67	68	69	70
71	72	73	74	75	76	77	78	79	80
81	82	83	84	85	86	87	88	89	90
91	92	93	94	95	96	97	98	99	100

Use the number square above to help you work out these probabilities.
Write your answers as fractions in their simplest forms.

A number is chosen at random between 1 and 100 (inclusive).
Work out the probability that the number is …

1. a multiple of 10
2. a multiple of 5
3. a multiple of 2
4. greater than 90
5. less than 5
6. greater than 5
7. between 20 and 30 (inclusive)
8. a two-digit number
9. a three-digit number
10. a factor of 50
11. a factor of 24
12. a factor of 11
13. a multiple of 11
14. a square number
15. an odd number
16. a multiple of 13
17. a power of 2
18. a multiple of 3
19. a triangle number
20. a prime number

Statements about Probability

1 Tomorrow either it will rain or it won't rain.
Therefore the probability of rain tomorrow is 50%.

2 Bag A contains 4 red counters and 2 blue counters.
Bag B contains 10 red counters and 7 blue counters.
If you pick a counter out of bag B, you are more likely to get a red counter than with bag A because there are more red counters in bag B.

3 If you throw a coin 50 times and you get 48 heads and only 2 tails the coin must be biased.

4 If you throw a coin 50 times you are more likely to get 26 heads and 24 tails than to get exactly 25 of each, because getting exactly 25 heads and 25 tails is pretty unlikely.

5 Everyone knows that some people are luckier than others.
And everyone has good days and bad days.
So the probability of getting a 6 with a dice depends on who throws it and when.
You can't just say it's always $\frac{1}{6}$.

6 I know someone who's practised with cards and can pull out an ace whenever he wants to.
So for him the probability of getting an ace is nothing to do with chance.

7 If you throw two dice the chance of getting a double 6 is less than the chance of getting a double 5 because a double 6 would be the maximum score possible and there's only one way of that happening.

8 If you buy two raffle tickets from different places in the book, you are more likely to win than if you buy two consecutive tickets.
Consecutive tickets would be very unlikely to come up.

9 Next-door is a family with 4 boys.
By the law of averages, the next child is bound to be a girl.

10 The probability of there being a bomb on an aeroplane is 1 in a million.
The probability of there being *two* bombs on an aeroplane is much smaller.
Therefore if I take a bomb with me I'm much less likely to get blown up by someone else's bomb!

Two Dice Horse Race

											FINISH ↓
1											
2											
3											
4											
5											
6											
7											
8											
9											
10											
11											
12											

Probability Summary

- **Event:** An **event** A, B, etc. is a possible outcome or a set of possible outcomes.
  e.g. A = throwing a fair dice and getting a 4,
  or B = throwing a fair dice and getting an even number.
  $n(A)$ is the number of equally likely ways of A happening.
  $n(\varepsilon)$ is the total number of equally likely outcomes (all the possibilities).
  $p(A)$ is the probability of A happening, so
  $$p(A) = \frac{n(A)}{n(\varepsilon)},$$
  and $p(A)$ must be between 0 (impossible, if there's no way of A happening) and 1 (certain, if A is the only thing that could happen).

- **The Complement of A:** This is the event "A doesn't happen".
  We use the symbol A'. E.g., if A = throwing a fair dice and getting a 4,
  then A' = throwing a fair dice and *not* getting a 4.
  It's always true that $p(A') = 1 - p(A)$.
  Sometimes if you want $p(A)$ it's easier to calculate $p(A')$ and use this formula to get $p(A)$.
  E.g., if A = throwing two fair dice and getting a total of at least 3, then
  A' = throwing two fair dice and getting a total of 2, so $p(A) = 1 - \frac{1}{36} = \frac{35}{36}$.

- **Combined Events:** If you have two events A and B, then
  $$p(A \cup B) = p(A) + p(B) - p(A \cap B)$$
  $p(A \cup B)$ means the probability of *either* A *or* B happening (called "A **union** B")
  $p(A \cap B)$ means the probability of *both* A *and* B happening ("A **intersection** B")
  $p(A)$ includes the chance of A and B both happening [$p(A \cap B)$].
  $p(B)$ also includes the chance of A and B both happening [$p(A \cap B)$],
  so $p(A) + p(B)$ includes $2 \times p(A \cap B)$, and that's why we have to subtract $p(A \cap B)$ in the formula above (so we don't count it twice).
  You can see all of this more clearly on a **Venn diagram**.

- **Mutually Exclusive Events:** If A and B *cannot both* happen together (one excludes the possibility of the other), they're called **mutually exclusive** events.
  In that case $p(A \cap B) = 0$, so the formula above simplifies to
  $$p(A \cup B) = p(A) + p(B).$$
  But remember you can add probabilities like this only if they're mutually exclusive.

- **Conditional Probability:** We write $p(B|A)$ for the probability that B happens *given that* A *has already happened*. This is what you see on the 2nd branch of a **tree diagram**.
  You can only get there by going along the 1st branch, so A must already have happened.
  The probability that A happens and then B happens is
  $$p(A \cap B) = p(A) \times p(B|A).$$
  You can also write this formula as $p(B|A) = \dfrac{p(A \cap B)}{p(A)}$.

- **Independent Events:** If B is independent of A then it doesn't make any difference whether A happens or A' happens. In that case,
  $$p(B|A) = p(B|A') = p(B)$$
  Therefore $p(A \cap B) = p(A) \times p(B)$, but you must remember to use this only when events A and B are independent.

Sample Space Diagrams

A Total of Numbers on Two 6-Sided Dice

Let X = total score

	1	2	3	4	5	6
1	2	3	4	5	6	7
2	3	4	5	6	7	8
3	4	5	6	7	8	9
4	5	6	7	8	9	10
5	6	7	8	9	10	11
6	7	8	9	10	11	12

X	$p(X)$
1	0
2	$\frac{1}{36}$
3	$\frac{1}{18}$
4	$\frac{1}{12}$
5	$\frac{1}{9}$
6	$\frac{5}{36}$
7	$\frac{1}{6}$
8	$\frac{5}{36}$
9	$\frac{1}{9}$
10	$\frac{1}{12}$
11	$\frac{1}{18}$
12	$\frac{1}{36}$
total	1

B Difference of Numbers on Two 6-Sided Dice

Let X = difference of scores

	1	2	3	4	5	6
1	0	1	2	3	4	5
2	1	0	1	2	3	4
3	2	1	0	1	2	3
4	3	2	1	0	1	2
5	4	3	2	1	0	1
6	5	4	3	2	1	0

X	$p(X)$
0	$\frac{1}{6}$
1	$\frac{5}{18}$
2	$\frac{2}{9}$
3	$\frac{1}{6}$
4	$\frac{1}{9}$
5	$\frac{1}{18}$
total	1

Three Dice Experiment

total	combination	no. of ways	total no. of ways	probability
3	1, 1, 1	1	1	$\frac{1}{216}$
4	1, 1, 2	3	3	$\frac{1}{72}$
5	1, 1, 3	3		
	1, 2, 2	3	6	$\frac{1}{36}$
6	1, 1, 4	3		
	1, 2, 3	6		
	2, 2, 2	1	10	$\frac{5}{108}$
7	1, 1, 5	3		
	1, 2, 4	6		
	1, 3, 3	3		
	2, 2, 3	3	15	$\frac{5}{72}$
8	1, 1, 6	3		
	1, 2, 5	6		
	1, 3, 4	6		
	2, 2, 4	3		
	2, 3, 3	3	21	$\frac{7}{72}$
9	1, 2, 6	6		
	1, 3, 5	6		
	1, 4, 4	3		
	2, 2, 5	3		
	2, 3, 4	6		
	3, 3, 3	1	25	$\frac{25}{216}$
10	1, 3, 6	6		
	1, 4, 5	6		
	2, 2, 6	3		
	2, 3, 5	6		
	2, 4, 4	3		
	3, 3, 4	3	27	$\frac{1}{8}$
11	1, 4, 6	6		
	1, 5, 5	3		
	2, 3, 6	6		
	2, 4, 5	6		
	3, 3, 5	3		
	3, 4, 4	3	27	$\frac{1}{8}$
12	1, 5, 6	6		
	2, 4, 6	6		
	2, 5, 5	3		
	3, 3, 6	3		
	3, 4, 5	6		
	4, 4, 4	1	25	$\frac{25}{216}$
13	1, 6, 6	3		
	2, 5, 6	6		
	3, 4, 6	6		
	3, 5, 5	3		
	4, 4, 5	3	21	$\frac{7}{72}$
14	2, 6, 6	3		
	3, 5, 6	6		
	4, 4, 6	3		
	4, 5, 5	3	15	$\frac{5}{72}$
15	3, 6, 6	3		
	4, 5, 6	6		
	5, 5, 5	1	10	$\frac{5}{108}$
16	4, 6, 6	3		
	5, 5, 6	3	6	$\frac{1}{36}$
17	5, 6, 6	3	3	$\frac{1}{72}$
18	6, 6, 6	1	1	$\frac{1}{216}$
total			216	1

Instant Maths Ideas: 3

Paving Slabs Investigation

1. Measure and record the length of the stick you are using.
2. Drop the stick onto the squared "paving slabs" area.
   The stick may fall more "randomly" if you gently throw it upwards and let it fall back to the paper.
3. Record the number of times the stick falls across a line for 100 throws.
4. Work out the *relative frequency* of "hits".
5. What information does this answer give you?

Working Out Probabilities

There are different ways of arriving at probabilities.

	Method	*Example*	*Exact or Estimate?*
1	**Experiment** Do it lots of times, calculate the *relative frequency* and use that as an estimate for the probability.	Finding the probability of a drawing pin landing with its point upwards.	Estimate.
2	**Research** Use data already collected by someone else to calculate the *relative frequency* and use that as an estimate for the probability.	Finding the probability of someone who is left-handed passing their driving test first time.	Estimate.
3	**Personal Judgment** Give your best guess for the particular circumstances.	Finding the probability that a particular person will eat chips for lunch tomorrow.	Estimate.
4	**Theory** Decide that some outcomes ought to be equally likely and divide the number of equally likely ways it could happen by the total number of ways.	Finding the probability of throwing a 5 with a normal dice.	Exact if our assumptions are valid.

Think of some more examples for each of the four methods.

What are the advantages and disadvantages of each method?

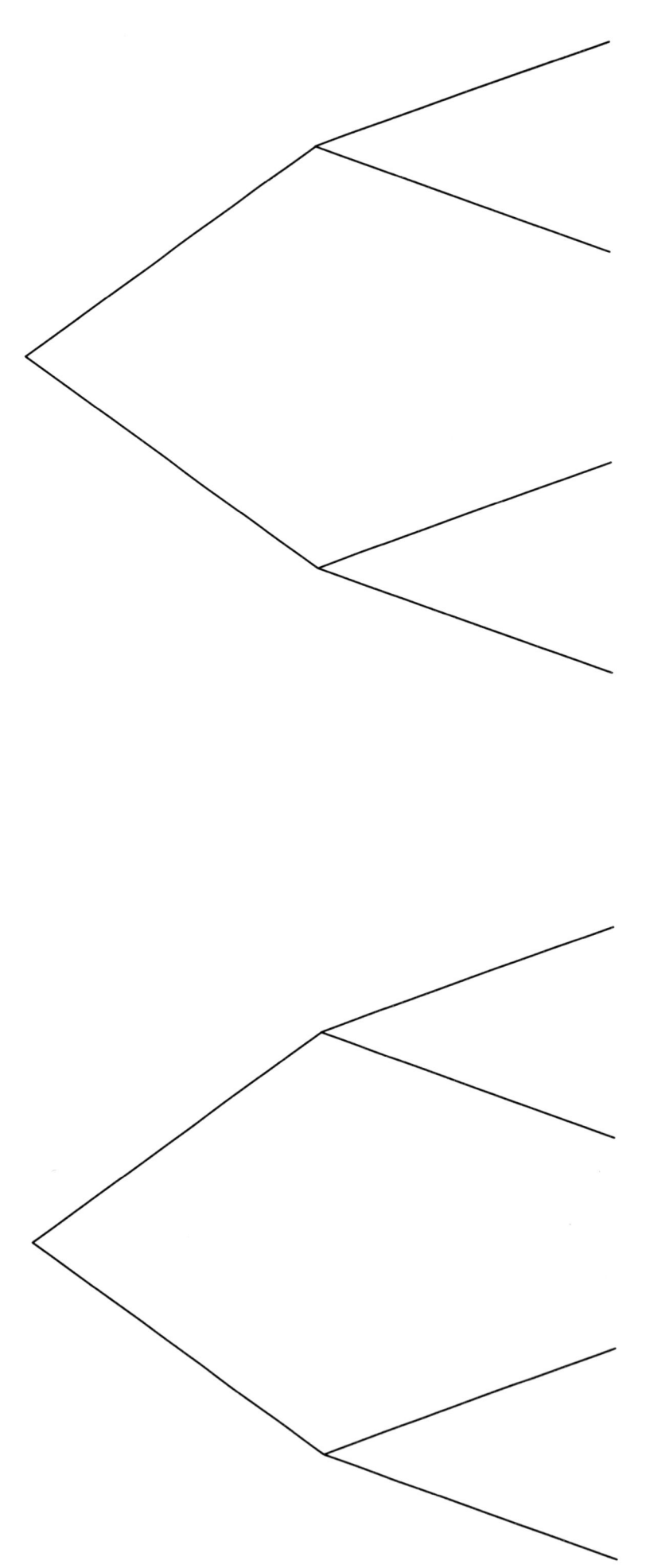

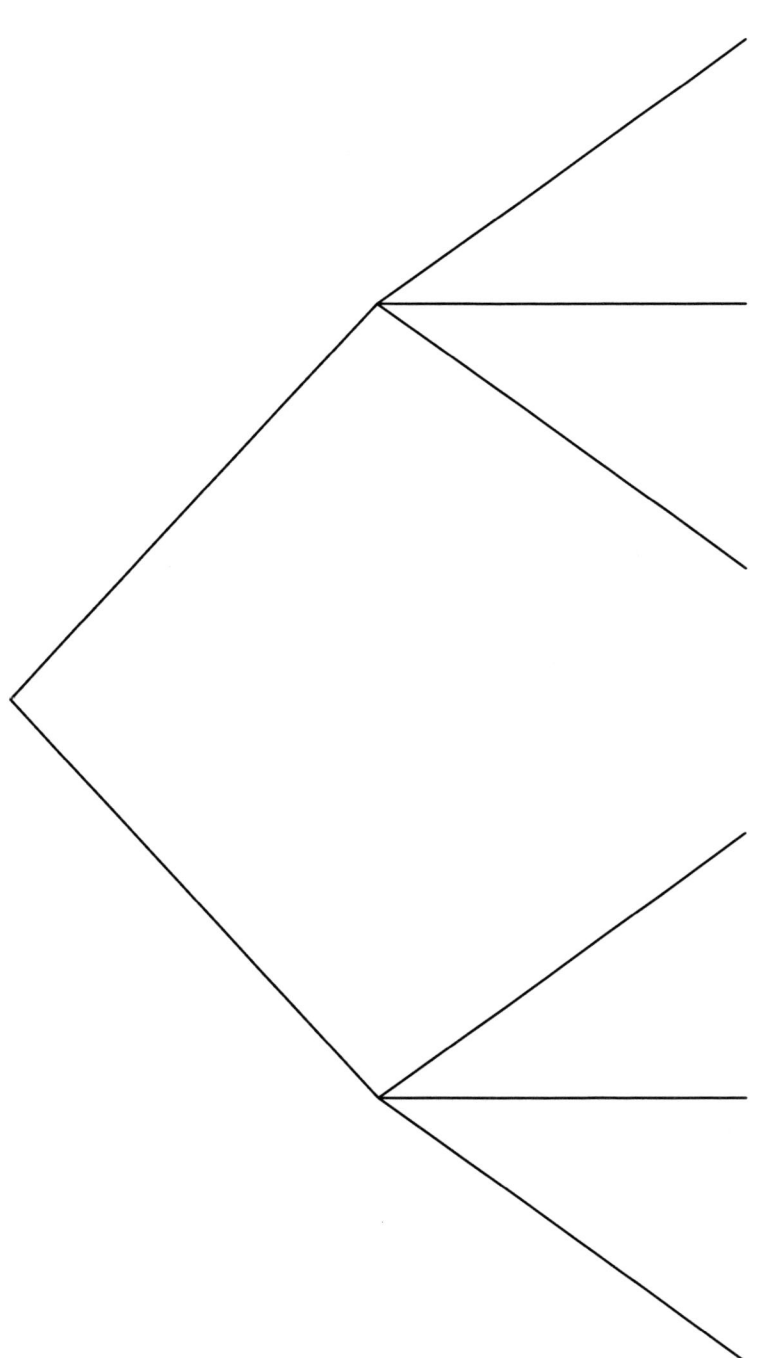

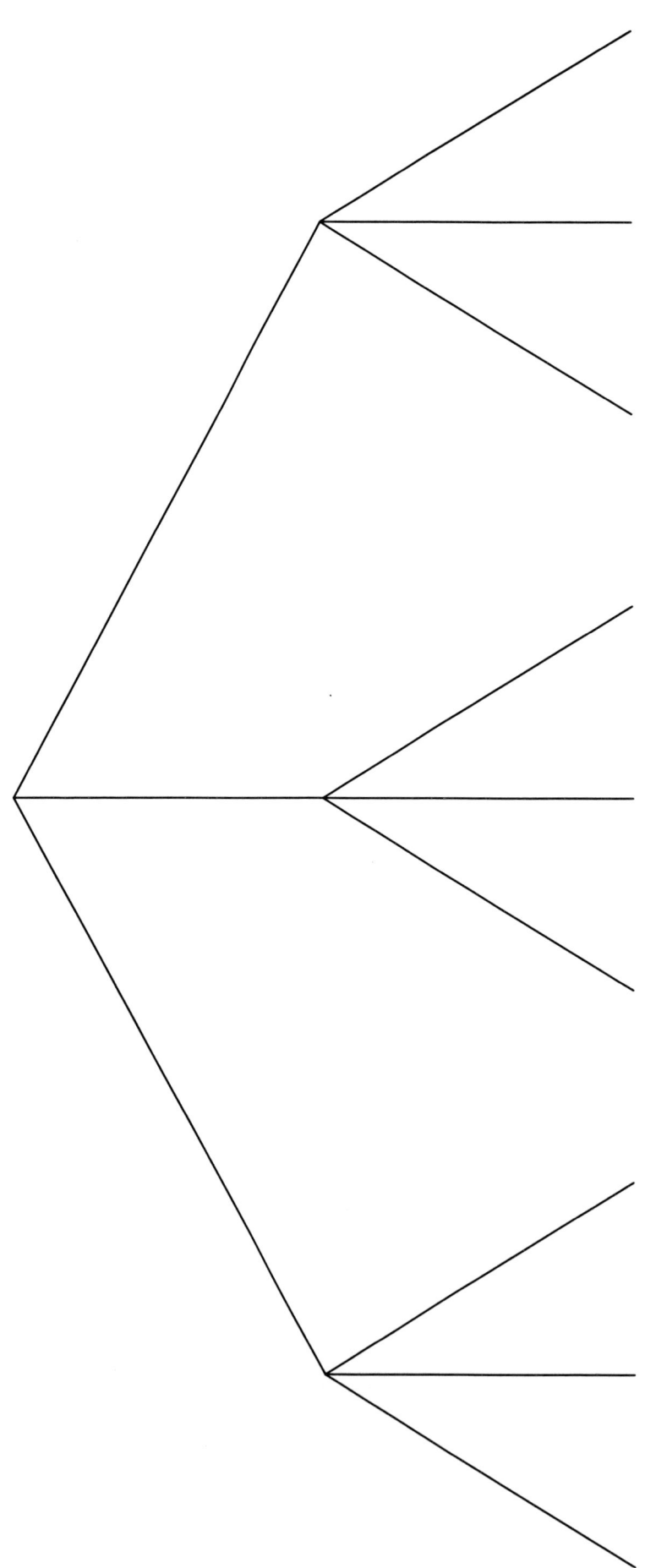

3.6 Numeracy Ideas

- These ideas vary considerably in content and length of time necessary. Some might be useful as lesson starters/finishers. Others could develop into a whole lesson's work. Some would operate well as homework tasks. They are presented below in no particular order (deliberately, so as to promote some variety if you are working your way through them).
- Some tasks may become favourites with pupils and can be used again and again; others will just become boring if over-used: it's a matter for your judgement.

3.6.1 **NEED** acetate of one or more of the "Number Grids" pages.
Put one up on an OHP (this is economical, because you can use the same ones again and again). Pupils draw a 4 × 4 grid (make the squares reasonably large). When everyone's ready, issue a rule, e.g., "double it", or "divide by 100" and pupils write out the answers against the clock.

There are endless possibilities; e.g., rounding, finding the mean of a column, factors (with integers), etc.

Various grids are given:
1. *Positive integers*
2. *Positive and negative integers*
3. *Positive decimals*
4. *Positive and negative decimals*
5. *Fractions*
6. *Percentages*

Or you can use the grids orally – pointing at a number, say, "what's 100 take away this one", "what's the nearest prime number to this one", etc.

3.6.2 Can you make 100 out of four nines?

Answer: $99 + \frac{9}{9}$ *or [99.99], where brackets indicate rounding to the nearest integer.*

3.6.3 By adding 1 straight line to this, make it true.
10 10 10 = 9.50

Answer: 10 TO 10 = 9.50
("ten minutes to ten")

3.6.4 Using the digits 1 to 9 once each, *in order*, how can you make 100?

Answers: lots of ways!
$1 + 2 + 3 + 4 + 5 + 6 + 7 + 8 \times 9 = 100$
$1 + 2 + 3 - 4 + 5 + 6 + 78 + 9 = 100$
$123 - 4 - 5 - 6 - 7 + 8 - 9 = 100$
$1 + 2 \times 3 + 4 \times 5 - 6 + 7 + 8 \times 9 = 100$
$12 + 34 - 5 + 6 + 7 + 8 - 9 = 100$
and many more!

3.6.5 A nine-digit number has all its digits different. When it's multiplied by 8, the answer again has nine digits, all of them different. What are the numbers?

Answer: $123456789 \times 8 = 987654312$
(Notice the order of the final two digits.)

3.6.6 What **word** goes in the gap?
"This sentence has _____ letters."
e.g., the word "thirteen" won't do, because the sentence would have 30 letters.

Answer: "thirty-one" or "thirty-three"

Don't count a space or a full stop as a "letter".

3.6.7 **NEED** acetate of musical composers and the accompanying sheet.
Mental number work together with getting information from a list.

Pupils could research a version involving famous mathematicians or other famous people of interest to them. (With modern-day celebrities who are still alive, pupils could make up something based on their dates of birth.) The internet is ideal for collecting this sort of information.

Instant Maths Ideas: 3

3.6.8 **NEED** acetate of price list from the school canteen
"How much would it cost for …?"
"How much change would I get from a £5 note if I bought …?", etc.

3.6.9 Missing Digits.

1. Addition/Subtraction; e.g., 43A + B4 = 5C1
   (usually best solved by writing in columns)
2. Multiplication
   (usually best solved by writing as long multiplication)
3. Division
   (usually best solved by converting into the equivalent multiplication problem)

Letters stand for digits (e.g., A = 7, B = 6, C = 0); within a question the same letter always represents the same digit.

Pupils can make these up. There will often be more than one possible answer.

You can play these like "hangman".

3.6.10 Target Numbers.
Pick four, five or six numbers, combine them in some way to make a "target number". Write the target number on the board in a circle.
e.g., numbers 11, 7, 3 and 9 and the target number is 35.

The rule can be either that you have to use all the numbers or that you don't.
Normal maths symbols like +, − , etc. are always allowed.

Answer: $11 \times 3 - 7 + 9 = 35$

Pupils may need to know BIDMAS, or you could use this task to introduce it.

You can use a today's date or a pupil's date of birth as the digits; e.g., 12th January 1992 gives 1, 2, 0, 1, 9, 2 (12/01/92) as the six numbers. Gradually work around the whole class.

You can choose any reasonable target number, since if it is impossible to make exactly then the winner will be the person who gets the nearest.

3.6.11 Mental Squares.
Draw this on the board.

1	2	3
4	5	6
7	8	9

You've got 15 seconds to memorise it, then I'm going to rub it off. Then I'm going to ask you some questions about it.

1. What number is in the middle?
2. Add up the right hand row.
3. Multiply the three numbers on the top row.

You can change the square by saying "Add 9 to the middle number. Now what is the total of the middle column?" or "Swap the numbers at the top right and bottom left. Now what is the total of the bottom row?", etc.

(Press hard with the board rubber so that the numbers don't still show!)

Some pupils may prefer to close their eyes when thinking about the questions.

You could write R and L on the right and left sides of the board to make the task accessible to pupils who muddle up the directions.

3.6.12
- Find a number which is increased by 12 when it's turned upside down.
- Find a number which is increased by 21 when it's turned upside down.
- Find a number which is twice the product of its digits.
- Find a number that is the same when turned upside down. How many are there?

Answers:
86
68

36

69, 6699, 88, 111, 101, etc.

3.6.13 Number Triangles (see sheets).

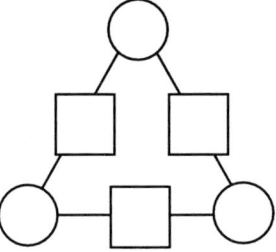

Generally you give the numbers in the square boxes and the task is to find what the numbers in the circles have to be.

There are different possible rules:

1. Addition:
   "Square number" = sum of the two adjacent "circle numbers";
2. Multiplication:
   "Square number" = product of the two adjacent "circle numbers".

3.6.14 Bingo.

Method 1 (quicker):
Draw a 5 × 5 square and fill it with the numbers from 1 to 25 (each one once each).
(It may be easiest to write them down in numerical order so that you know you haven't missed one.)
You need to get all 5 numbers in a row or a column or a diagonal to win. If an answer lies outside the range 1 to 25, ignore it (but don't say anything otherwise you'll help other people to win!).

Method 2 (longer):
Draw a 2 × 5 rectangle.
Choose 10 different integers between 1 and 50 and fill them into the 10 squares however you like.
You need to get a "full house" to win.
If an answer lies outside the range 1 to 50, ignore it.
(It's probably best not to allow repeated numbers, because it can cut the game very short; someone could win on the first question.)

You could give out prizes if you're feeling generous!

For "times tables bingo" you can have a bag containing small pieces of card with the numbers 1 to 12 written on (two of each number). You pull out two cards, and that's your multiplication. Try to vary the order in which you say the two numbers (e.g., "6 × 9" as well as "9 × 6") and use words like "product", "times", "multiply", "lots of", etc.

Easy to make up.

Methods of solution for the different rules:

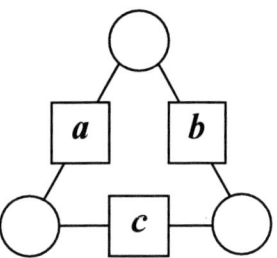

Once you have found one "circle number", the rest are easy to calculate.
So to find the "circle number" at the top,
1. *top number = $\frac{1}{2}(a+b-c)$;*
2. *top number = $\sqrt{\dfrac{ab}{c}}$, assuming that an odd number (one or three) of a, b and c are not negative, and that $c \neq 0$.*

Just normal mental number work; e.g.,

1. *a number of identical items of a certain value bought for a given total cost;*
2. *converting between units of length / area / volume, etc. (metric / imperial, etc.);*
3. *polygon or angle facts (e.g., "the number of degrees inside a quadrilateral divided by the number of sides in a hexagon all divided by 10");*
4. *powers and roots (e.g., "the cube root of 125 take-away the positive square root of 16");*
5. *multiples and factors (e.g., "the LCM of 12 and 8 divided by the HCF of 12 and 8");*
6. *decimal and fraction multiplication; percentages;*
7. *negative numbers;*
8. *square / triangle numbers, etc. (e.g., "the third cube number divided by the second triangle number");*
9. *algebra (e.g., "if $a=4$ and $b=10$, what is $ab-2b$");*
10. *inequalities (e.g., "if $2x>15$ and $x<9$, and x is an integer, what is x?"*
11. *mean, mode, median, range.*

If necessary, pupils can keep an eye on the people sitting near to them to make sure they don't alter their numbers once the game has started! It may be worth keeping a record of the answers to your questions in case of any dispute over which numbers have "gone".

A cloth money bag, available from banks, is ideal for this.

3.6.15 Numbers and Words (see sheet).
Answers:
Task 1:
You always eventually hit "four", which has 4 letters.

Task 2:
The largest I can do is FIVE THOUSAND.
The smallest I can do is MINUS FORTY.

Task 3:
The largest is 17 and the smallest is 1. In order they go 1, 10, 5, 9, 8, 6, 3, 2, 4, 11, 7, 15, 18, 19 12, 16, 13, 14, 20, 17 (smallest to largest).

This task is in danger of reinforcing the misconception that A always equals 1, B always equals 2, and so on. Yet this is an enjoyable activity which it would be a pity to omit.

Values close to 100: Equation (102), polygon (104), formulas (105) and mathematical (106) are all close.

(See sheet of strips of alphabet and code.)

Some suggested tasks to try to make this potentially dull topic more interesting.

A creative pupil could perhaps adapt task 1 to make a magic trick.

Pupils may be able to do better than these.

Word Values:

number	value	number	value
ONE	34	ELEVEN	63
TWO	58	TWELVE	87
THREE	56	THIRTEEN	99
FOUR	60	FOURTEEN	104
FIVE	42	FIFTEEN	65
SIX	52	SIXTEEN	96
SEVEN	65	SEVENTEEN	109
EIGHT	49	EIGHTEEN	73
NINE	42	NINETEEN	86
TEN	39	TWENTY	107

You can insist that words must be maths-related or not, as appropriate.

3.6.16 Integer Investigations (see sheet).
Answers:
Process 1:
You always get 1089.
4-digit numbers give 10890
5-digit numbers give 109890, and so on
(6 gives 1098900, 7 gives 10998900, etc.).

Process 2:
Within 6 steps you should reach 495.
This is Kaprekar's process (1905-1988).
With 4-digit numbers, you should reach 6174 within 7 steps.
It is very hard to explain completely why this happens.

Process 3:
e.g., 44 → 22 → 11 → 34 → 17 → 52 → 26 → 13 → 40 → 20 → 10 → 5 → 16 → 8 → 4 → 2 → 1.
You always end up with a loop that goes 4 → 2 → 1 → 4 → 2 → 1, etc. You get there quickly once you hit a power of 2 (e.g., from 16 above).
This is called Collatz's process (1910-1990).
No-one knows if you will always get to 1 whatever number you begin with.

Process 4:
You always end up at 4 eventually, because that's the only number which makes itself when you add 8 and divide by 3.
If $x_{n+1} = \dfrac{x_n + 8}{3}$, then $3x = x + 8$, so $x = 4$.

3.6.17 Un-magic Squares (see sheets).

Some interesting tasks involving integer arithmetic.

1089 Proof
If the original number is "abc", we can write that as $100a + 10b + c$, and we'll assume that $a > c$ so that this is bigger than its reverse.
The reverse number can be written $100c + 10b + a$, and when we subtract the smaller from the bigger we get $100(a-c) + (c-a) = 99(a-c)$, so at the first stage we will always get a multiple of 99.
Since $a > c$, the "units digit" $(c-a)$ is negative, so we have to break one of the hundreds into $90 + 10$. This gives $100(a-c-1) + 10 \times 9 + (10+c-a)$.
The units digit $(10+c-a)$ is now positive.
When we reverse this number we get $100(10+c-a) + 10 \times 9 + (a-c-1)$, and doing the addition gives us $100(10-1) + 2 \times 10 \times 9 + (10-1)$
$= 1089$.
This only works because we assumed that a, b and c were all different from each other.

In general, if the rule is "add a, divide by b", then the final number will be $\dfrac{a}{b-1}$. This won't work if $b \leq 1$, because the numbers in the sequence will just get bigger and bigger.

You can either use the sheets or just write a couple onto the board.

3.6.18 Boxes (see sheet).

(This idea also appears in section 3.7.6.)

A Fibonacci-type (1170-1250) investigation.

3.6.19 Picture Frames (see sheets).

These can be quite challenging. Pupils' own problems along these lines can be extremely difficult.

3.6.20 Biggest Products (see sheet).

This task can be used as an excuse to practise non-calculator multiplication (e.g., by the gelosia method – see section 1.5). It is a way of giving a larger purpose to some routine practice and also incorporates some logical thinking, possibly even some algebra.

3.6.21 Scoring 100 (see sheet).

Numeracy games suitable for playing in pairs. They are an opportunity to develop number skill but also to think about strategy.
Pupils enjoy being "in the know" and winning with ease once they know how!

3.6.22 Broken Calculator (see sheet).

It is an interesting task to consider which buttons on the calculator are "really essential" and which are just "convenient". There isn't a sharp distinction, since even trigonometrical functions can be evaluated using power series, but it is reasonable to say, for example, that we could manage with just the sin button and use identities like $\cos x = \sin(90 - x)$ to find $\cos$ of anything and then use $\tan x = \dfrac{\sin x}{\cos x}$ to find $\tan$ of anything.
Which other buttons could we manage without?

This is a non-calculator task!

Another way of putting it is "if you could have only five buttons beyond the numbers 0 to 9, what five would you choose?" *(It does depend to some extent on the kind of calculations the pupils would anticipate needing to do.)*
- Do two presses of the "minus" key work as addition?
- Do you need the decimal point AND the divide key?
- The power key can cover "squared" and all the roots.

This task makes you appreciate a fully-functional calculator!

3.6.23 Day of the Week (see sheet).

An interesting task involving careful following of instructions and simple number calculations.

Pupils may not know that British elections happen on Thursdays, but they should still be able to identify that one by a process of elimination.

Other dates that pupils/parents may remember the day of might include the following:
- assassination of President Kennedy:
    Friday 22 November 1963;
- Neil Armstrong stepping onto the moon:
    Monday 21 July 1969;
- wedding of Prince Charles and Lady Diana:
    Wednesday 29 July 1981;
- death of Princess Diana:
    Sunday 31 August 1997;
- terrorist attacks in US:
    Tuesday 11 September 2001.

Answers:
Obviously there may be links with material pupils are studying in History.

"Black Friday"	18 November 1910
"Bloody Sunday"	22 January 1905
"Black Wednesday"	16 September 1992
UK General Election	1 May 1997

1910 was the Suffragettes' demonstration outside the Houses of Parliament;
1905 was the Russian demonstration (not the Irish "Bloody Sunday");
1992 was the fall of the pound from the exchange rate mechanism;
1997 was the big Labour win.

Positive Integers

31	22	17	44	6
10	57	2	26	68
79	72	45	12	0
94	3	63	1	19
81	20	98	5	38

Positive and Negative Integers

4	2	12	−1
1	−7	32	−16
−3	28	0	−5
26	−2	15	−30

Instant Maths Ideas: 3

Positive Decimals

0.01	3.5	2.08	3.17
5.6	0	4.3	0.25
5.08	1.3	6.2	0.1
2.8	10.3	1.99	4.95

Positive and Negative Decimals

0.3	1.83	6.66	−0.12
0.9	−3.55	0	4.4
1.7	−0.05	5.9	−0.1
−2.06	−10.3	−5.37	2.61

Fractions

$\dfrac{2}{3}$	$\dfrac{9}{10}$	$\dfrac{1}{6}$	$\dfrac{2}{5}$
$\dfrac{10}{21}$	$\dfrac{1}{2}$	$\dfrac{5}{8}$	$\dfrac{3}{4}$
$\dfrac{4}{5}$	$\dfrac{5}{6}$	$\dfrac{2}{11}$	$\dfrac{1}{3}$
$\dfrac{1}{4}$	$\dfrac{4}{9}$	$\dfrac{3}{5}$	$\dfrac{99}{100}$

Percentages

20%	**15%**	**11%**	**75%**
24%	**7%**	**1%**	**30%**
2%	**65%**	**50%**	**80%**
60%	**40%**	**5%**	**25%**

Bach	1685-1750
Handel	1685-1759
Haydn	1732-1809
Mozart	1756-1791
Beethoven	1770-1827
Schubert	1797-1828
Mendelssohn	1809-1847
Chopin	1810-1849
Schumann	1810-1856

Musical Composers — **TEACHER'S NOTES**

Bach	**1685-1750**
Handel	**1685-1759**
Haydn	**1732-1809**
Mozart	**1756-1791**
Beethoven	**1770-1827**
Schubert	**1797-1828**
Mendelssohn	**1809-1847**
Chopin	**1810-1849**
Schumann	**1810-1856**

Cover up left side: "What do you think these numbers are?"
(Are they likely to be take-away sums? What makes them look like dates?, etc.)

Say that it's OK for pupils to abbreviate the composers' names when writing their answers, so long as they find a way of distinguishing between names that start with the same letter.

1	How long did Bach live?	***65 years***
2	How long did Haydn live for after Mozart had died?	***18 years***
3	Which people on the list could Mozart have met if they'd been in the same place?	***Handel, Haydn, Beethoven***
4	How much longer did Handel live than Beethoven?	***17 years longer***
5	Who lived the longest?	***Haydn***
6	Who died the youngest?	***Schubert***
7	When will it be the 300th anniversary of Haydn's birth?	***In 2032***
8	We were all born in the 20th century and we'll probably all die in the 21st century. Which people on the list were like us – born in one century and died in the next?	***Bach, Handel, Haydn, Beethoven, Schubert***
9	Which composer lived 1 year longer than another one on the list?	***Chopin (1 year longer than Mendelssohn)***
10	I'm going to tell you about a composer who *isn't* on the list. His name is Wagner and he lived twice as long as Mozart. He was born in 1813. When did he die?	***1883***

Number Triangles (Addition)

The number in each square is the *sum* of the numbers in the two circles connected to it.

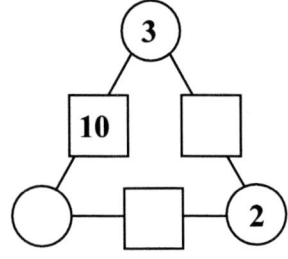 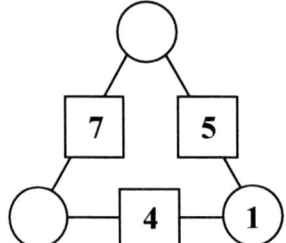 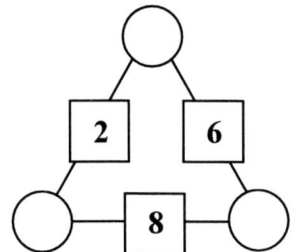

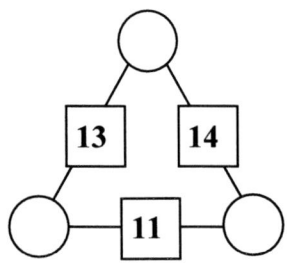 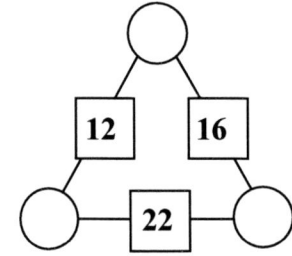 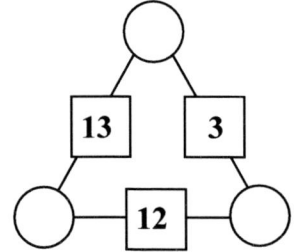

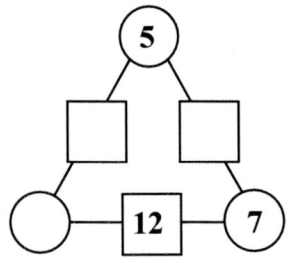 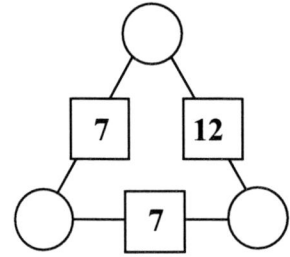 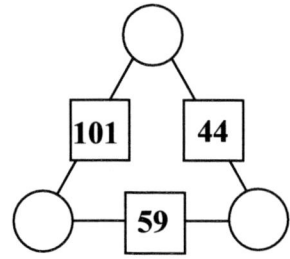

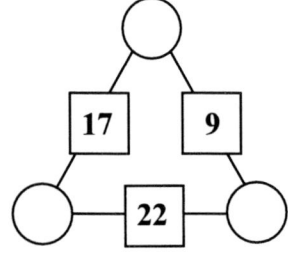 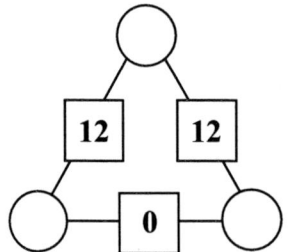 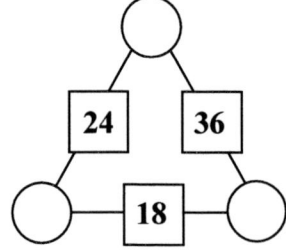

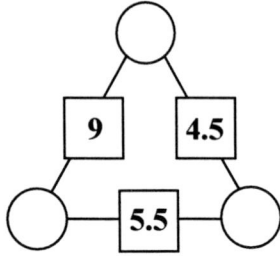 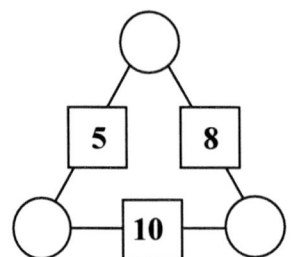 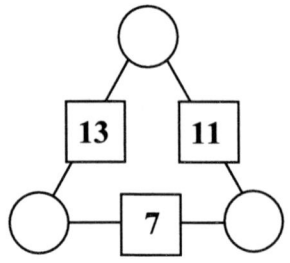

Number Triangles (Addition) ANSWERS

The number in each square is the *sum* of the numbers in the two circles connected to it.

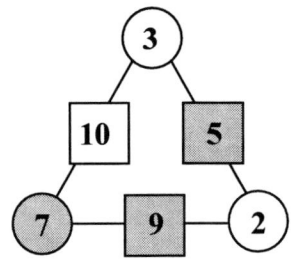 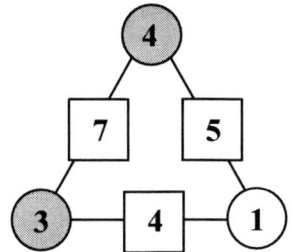 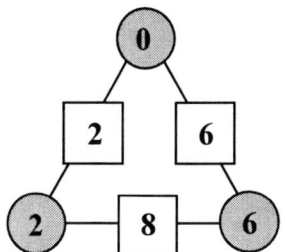

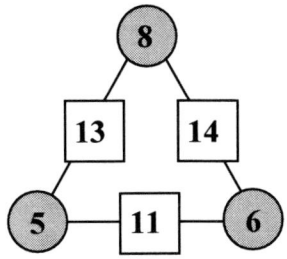 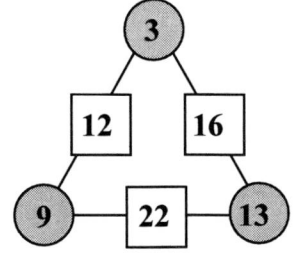 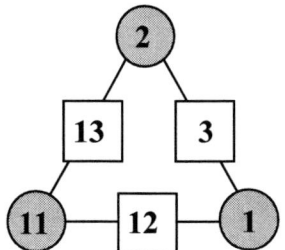

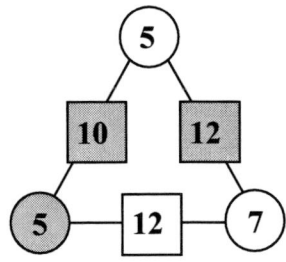 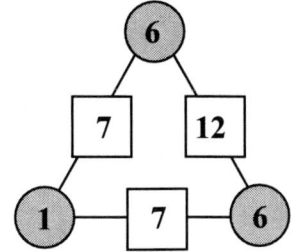 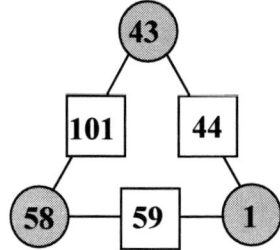

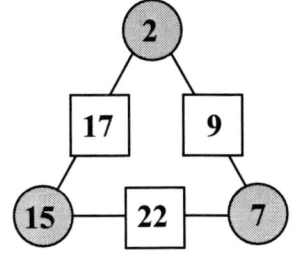 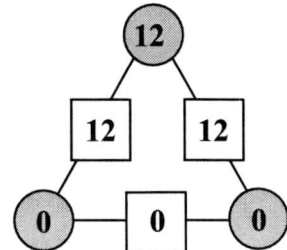 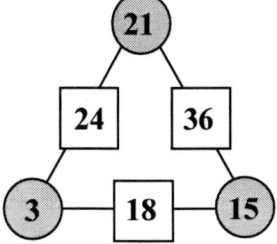

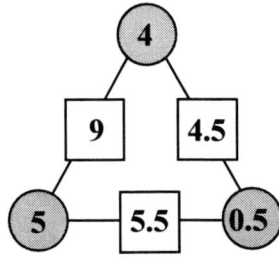 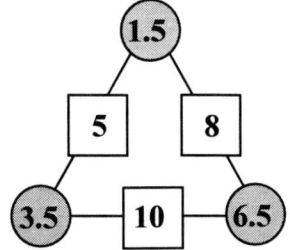 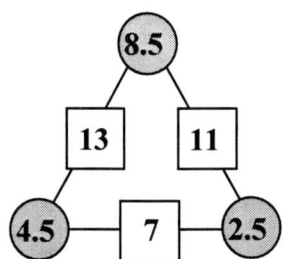

Instant Maths Ideas: 3

Number Triangles (Multiplication)

The number in each square is the *product (multiplication)* of the numbers in the two circles connected to it.

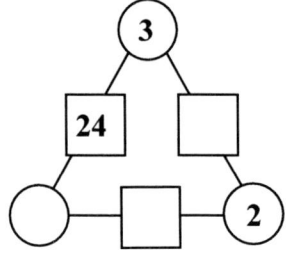 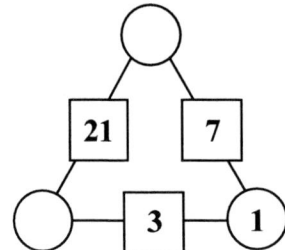 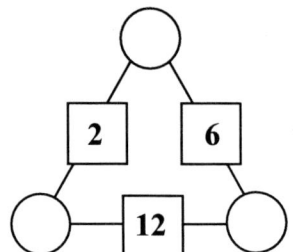

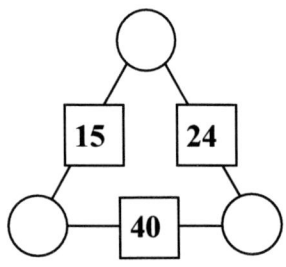 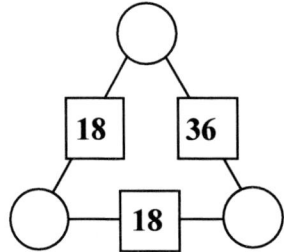 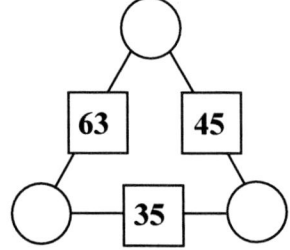

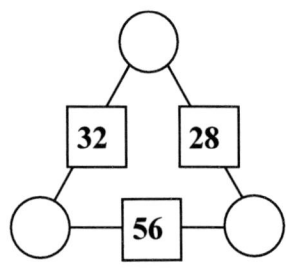 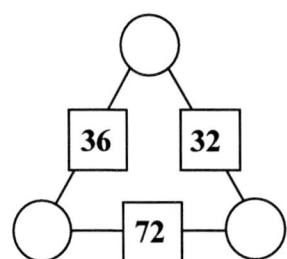 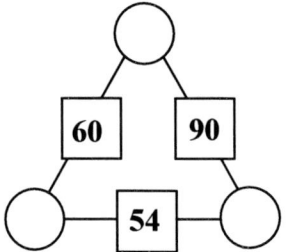

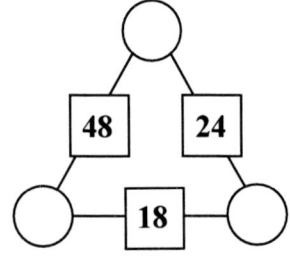 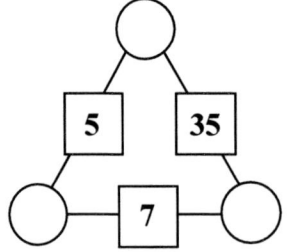 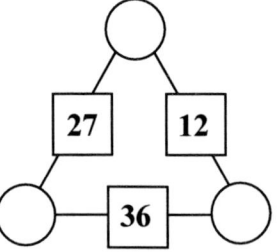

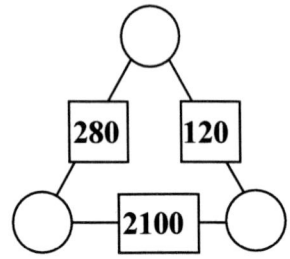 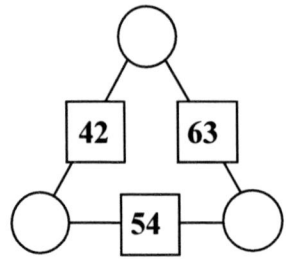 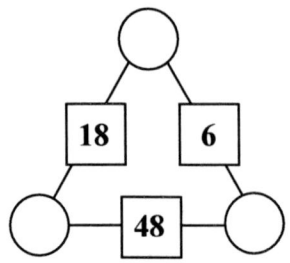

Number Triangles (Multiplication) ANSWERS

The number in each square is the *product (multiplication)* of the numbers in the two circles connected to it.

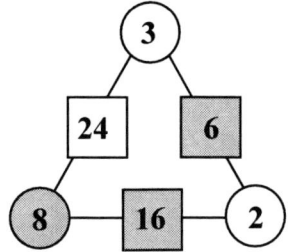 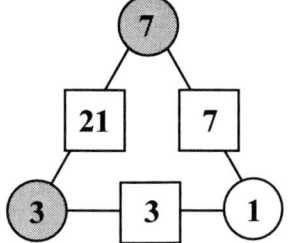 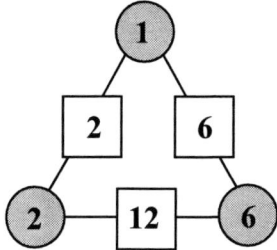

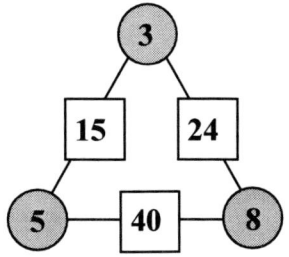 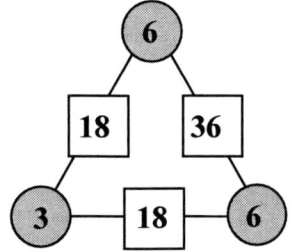 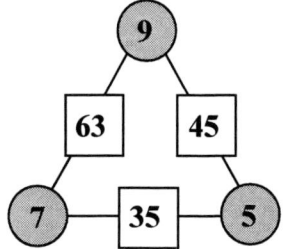

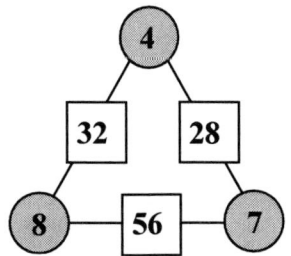 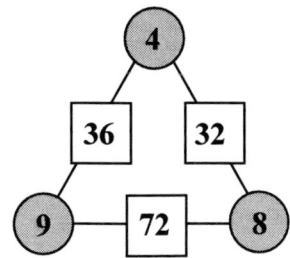 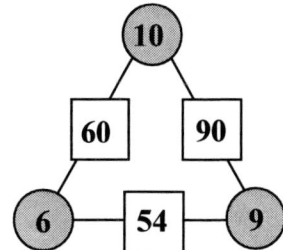

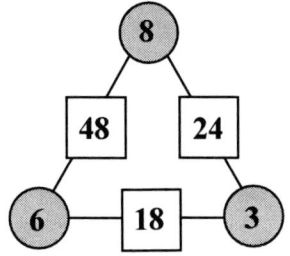 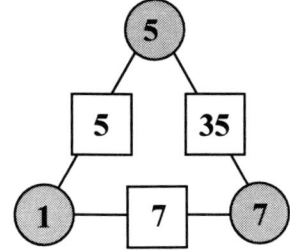 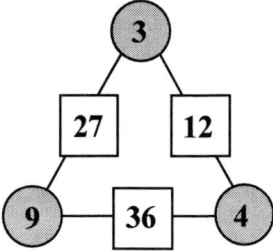

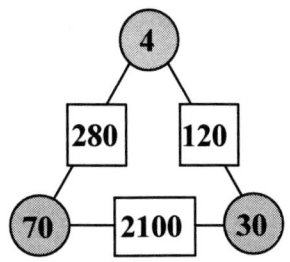 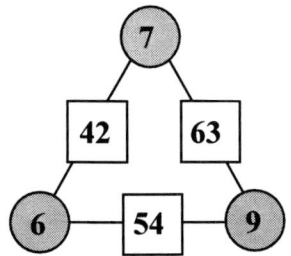 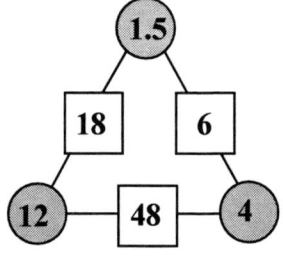

Instant Maths Ideas: 3

Numbers and Words

Remember that there is no "U" in FORTY.

Task 1

Choose an integer between 1 and 100 and write it in words; *e.g., thirty-eight*

Count up the total number of letters; *e.g., 11*

Write this number in words; *e.g., eleven*

Keep going; *e.g., six, three, ...*

What happens eventually?

Try it with some different starting numbers.

Can you explain why this happens?

Task 2

The three letters in the word *ten* are all different.
What is the largest number you can write in words where all the letters are different? You can use any letters you like, but you can use each letter only once.

What is the smallest number you can do?

Task 3

Let A = 1, B = 2, C = 3, etc. for this task.

For a word, like MATHS, the value is the *sum* of the values of the letters that make it up.
    e.g., for MATHS, 13 + 1 + 20 + 8 + 19 = 61.

Which 5-letter word has the biggest total?
It has to be a proper word.

Which has the smallest total?

Which number (in words) between *one* and *twenty* do you expect to have the biggest value? Which do you think would have the smallest?
Try it and see.

Write the numbers *one* to *twenty* in order of their word values.

Find a word with a value as close to 100 as you can.

A	B	C	D	E	F	G	H	I	J	K	L	M	N	O	P	Q	R	S	T	U	V	W	X	Y	Z
1	2	3	4	5	6	7	8	9	10	11	12	13	14	15	16	17	18	19	20	21	22	23	24	25	26

A	B	C	D	E	F	G	H	I	J	K	L	M	N	O	P	Q	R	S	T	U	V	W	X	Y	Z
1	2	3	4	5	6	7	8	9	10	11	12	13	14	15	16	17	18	19	20	21	22	23	24	25	26

A	B	C	D	E	F	G	H	I	J	K	L	M	N	O	P	Q	R	S	T	U	V	W	X	Y	Z
1	2	3	4	5	6	7	8	9	10	11	12	13	14	15	16	17	18	19	20	21	22	23	24	25	26

A	B	C	D	E	F	G	H	I	J	K	L	M	N	O	P	Q	R	S	T	U	V	W	X	Y	Z
1	2	3	4	5	6	7	8	9	10	11	12	13	14	15	16	17	18	19	20	21	22	23	24	25	26

A	B	C	D	E	F	G	H	I	J	K	L	M	N	O	P	Q	R	S	T	U	V	W	X	Y	Z
1	2	3	4	5	6	7	8	9	10	11	12	13	14	15	16	17	18	19	20	21	22	23	24	25	26

A	B	C	D	E	F	G	H	I	J	K	L	M	N	O	P	Q	R	S	T	U	V	W	X	Y	Z
1	2	3	4	5	6	7	8	9	10	11	12	13	14	15	16	17	18	19	20	21	22	23	24	25	26

Integer Investigations

Try these processes and see what happens in each case.
Follow the instructions carefully.

Process 1

		example
1	Choose any 3-digit number where all the digits are different.	*375*
2	Write down the digits in the opposite order.	*573*
3	Subtract the smaller from the larger.	*573 – 375 = 198*
4	Write down the digits of this new number in the opposite order.	*891*
5	Add these last two numbers.	*198 + 891 = 1089*

Try some more numbers.
Describe what happens.
Can you explain why?
What if you start with a 4-digit or 5-digit number?

Process 2

		example
1	Choose a 3-digit number where all the digits are different.	*452*
2	Arrange the digits so that they go from biggest to smallest (left to right).	*542*
3	Arrange the digits so that they go from smallest to biggest.	*245*
4	Subtract the second one from the first one.	*542 – 245 = 297*
5	Repeat using the new number.	
6	Keep going until you have a good reason to stop.	

Describe what happens.
Can you explain why?
Try it with 4-digit numbers.

Integer Investigations (continued)

Try these processes and see what happens in each case.
Follow the instructions carefully.

Process 3

example

1 Choose any 2-digit number. $38 \to 19 \to 58 \to 29 \to 88 \to$ *etc.*

2 If the number is even, divide by 2.

3 If the number is odd, multiply by 3 and add 1.

4 Go back to step 2.

5 Keep going until you have a good reason to stop.

Describe what happens.
Can you explain why?

Process 4

	example
1 Choose any integer between 1 and 100.	*47*
2 Add 8.	*55*
3 Divide the answer by 3. (If you get a decimal, that's OK.)	*18.333...*
4 Go back to step 2.	*26.333...*
5 Keep going until you have a good reason to stop.	*8.778..., etc.*

Describe what happens.
Can you explain why?

Make up a similar rule.
What happens this time?

Instant Maths Ideas: 3

Un-Magic Squares!

In a *magic square*, all the rows, all the columns and both diagonals add up to the same amount (the magic total).

The squares below are **un-magic squares**; there's *one wrong number* in each one.

Find the wrong number and correct it.

11	26	5
8	14	20
23	2	18

magic total =

12	22	20
25	18	10
16	14	24

magic total =

96	19	74
41	59	85
52	107	30

magic total =

38	93	16
27	49	71
82	6	60

magic total =

43	52	15
8	36	64
57	22	29

magic total =

28	24	45
48	32	16
20	40	36

magic total =

29	44	23
26	32	38
41	21	35

magic total =

25	20	21
18	22	26
32	24	19

magic total =

21	35	25
31	27	23
29	19	34

magic total =

147	143	163
167	151	153
139	159	155

magic total =

153	104	181
170	148	126
115	192	137

magic total =

289	224	237
197	250	302
263	276	211

magic total =

Un-Magic Squares!

In a *magic square*, all the rows, all the columns and both diagonals add up to the same amount (the magic total).
The squares below are **un**-magic squares; there's *one wrong number* in each one.
Find the wrong number and correct it.

One way of working is to write the totals of each row/column/diagonal round the edge. Sometimes you may notice the incorrect number because it is the only odd or only even number.

The shaded boxes are the corrected numbers, and the magic totals are in bold underneath.

11	26	5
8	14	20
23	2	**17**

magic total = **42**

12	22	20
26	18	10
16	14	24

magic total = **54**

96	19	74
41	**63**	85
52	107	30

magic total = **189**

38	93	16
27	49	71
82	**5**	60

magic total = **147**

43	**50**	15
8	36	64
57	22	29

magic total = **108**

28	24	**44**
48	32	16
20	40	36

magic total = **96**

29	44	23
26	32	38
41	**20**	35

magic total = **96**

25	20	21
18	22	26
23	24	19

magic total = **66**

21	35	25
31	27	23
29	19	**33**

magic total = **81**

147	143	163
167	151	**135**
139	159	155

magic total = **453**

159	104	181
170	148	126
115	192	137

magic total = **444**

289	224	237
198	250	302
263	276	211

magic total = **750**

Instant Maths Ideas: 3

Boxes   **TEACHER'S NOTES AND ANSWERS**

Draw a line of 5 boxes on the board with the numbers 3 and 4 in the first two boxes.

3	4			

The rule is that from the third number onwards, the number in each box is the sum of the *two* previous numbers. (Note, *not* the sum of *all* the previous numbers, just the previous *two*.)
(It's clearer to use the word "previous" because the "last" number may be taken to mean the number in the far right box.)
So we get

3	4	7	11	18

Doing it this way is pretty easy, but if I just gave you

3				18

and you had to find the missing numbers it would be much harder.

Try these. You can assume that all the numbers are positive integers, and that the number in the second box is larger than the number in the first box.

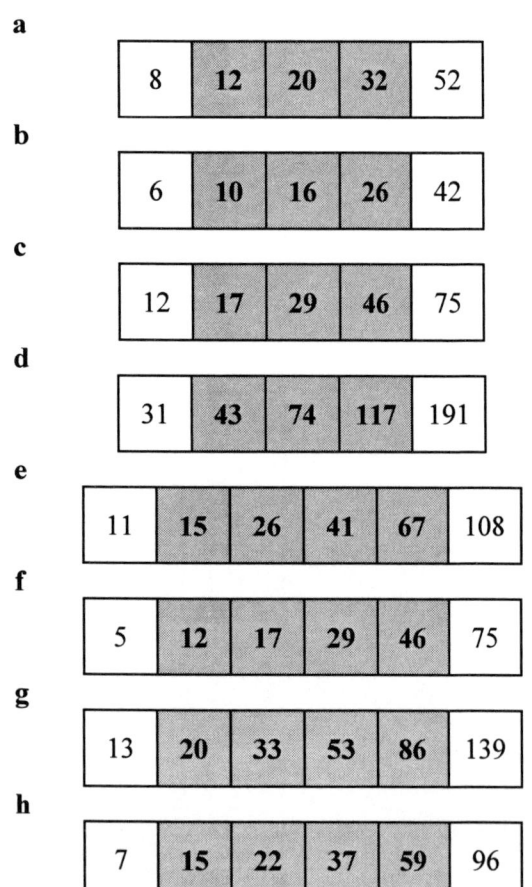

If instead I gave you

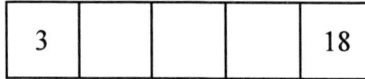

are there any other possibilities (apart from the previous solution)? No.

What if I just gave you

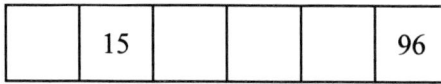

How many possible answers are there where all the numbers are positive integers?

The only other possibility where the 2nd number is bigger than the 1st is
2, 18, 20, 38, 58, 96.
If the 2nd number can be smaller than the 1st, then you can also have
2, 12, 24, 36, 60, 96;
22, 6, 28, 34, 62, 96;
27, 3, 30, 33, 63, 96;
32, 0, 32, 32, 64, 96.

Using algebra, if x and y are the integers in the first two boxes respectively ($y > x$), then the number in the fifth box will be $2x+3y$, and the number in the sixth box will be $3x+5y$.
(The co-efficients are the numbers from the Fibonacci sequence.) So you can repeatedly subtract 3 from 96, checking each time whether you have a multiple of 5;
e.g., $96 - 7 \times 3 = 75 = 15 \times 5$, so x can be 7 and y can be 15 (the original set of boxes).

Picture Frames

A rectangular picture frame is broken into straight pieces.
The lengths of the pieces are measured.
How should the pieces be fitted back together to make the original picture frame?

The first 5 were *square* picture frames.

lengths of pieces of picture frame (inches)

1   1, 1, 2, 2, 2, 3, 4, 5

2   1, 4, 6, 6, 8, 11, 12

3   1, 3, 4, 4, 5, 6, 6, 7, 7, 7, 10

4   10, 20, 30, 40, 50, 60, 70, 80

5   2, 2, 3, 3, 4, 5, 6, 10, 12, 14, 15

Rectangular picture frames are harder.
Try these.

lengths of pieces of picture frame (inches)

6   1, 1, 2, 3, 4, 4, 7

7   2, 2, 3, 3, 4, 4, 5, 7

8   1, 1, 2, 4, 4, 5, 7

9   2, 4, 5, 5, 6, 7, 7

10   1, 2, 3, 3, 6, 8, 9, 12

11   3, 3, 4, 5, 7, 10, 10, 10

12   1, 2, 2, 2, 3, 3, 6, 7

13   3, 3, 4, 4, 4, 4, 5, 11, 14

14   5, 6, 7, 8, 10, 10, 10, 12, 14

15   4, 4, 5, 6, 6, 7, 7, 8, 15

Can you invent a systematic way of solving problems like these?

Picture Frames

A rectangular picture frame is broken into straight pieces.
The lengths of the pieces are measured.
How should the pieces be fitted back together to make the original picture frame?

The first 5 were *square* picture frames.
Here you can add up the lengths of all the pieces and divide by 4 to find out how long the sides have to be.

	lengths of pieces of picture frame (inches)	length of sides (inches)	
1	1, 1, 2, 2, 2, 3, 4, 5	1 + 2 + 2 1 + 4	2 + 3 5
2	1, 4, 6, 6, 8, 11, 12	1 + 11 4 + 8	6 + 6 12
3	1, 3, 4, 4, 5, 6, 6, 7, 7, 7, 10	1 + 7 + 7 3 + 6 + 6	4 + 4 + 7 5 + 10
4	10, 20, 30, 40, 50, 60, 70, 80	10 + 80 20 + 70	30 + 60 40 + 50
5	2, 2, 3, 3, 4, 5, 6, 10, 12, 14, 15	2 + 3 + 14 2 + 5 + 12	3 + 6 + 10 4 + 15

Rectangular picture frames are harder.
Try these.

	lengths of pieces of picture frame (inches)	longer sides (inches)	shorter sides (inches)
6	1, 1, 2, 3, 4, 4, 7	1 + 7 4 + 4	1 + 2 3
7	2, 2, 3, 3, 4, 4, 5, 7	2 + 7 4 + 5	2 + 4 3 + 3
8	1, 1, 2, 4, 4, 5, 7	1 + 2 + 4 7	1 + 4 5
9	2, 4, 5, 5, 6, 7, 7	4 + 7 5 + 6	2 + 5 7
10	1, 2, 3, 3, 6, 8, 9, 12	1 + 12 2 + 3 + 8	3 + 6 9
11	3, 3, 4, 5, 7, 10, 10, 10	3 + 3 + 10 4 + 5 + 7	10 10
12	1, 2, 2, 2, 3, 3, 6, 7	2 + 7 3 + 6	1 + 3 2 + 2
13	3, 3, 4, 4, 4, 4, 5, 11, 14	3 + 4 + 11 4 + 14	3 + 5 4 + 4
14	5, 6, 7, 8, 10, 10, 10, 12, 14	6 + 10 + 10 12 + 14	5 + 10 7 + 8
15	4, 4, 5, 6, 6, 7, 7, 8, 15	4 + 15 5 + 7 + 7	4 + 8 6 + 6

There may be other possible answers.

Biggest Products **TEACHER'S NOTES AND ANSWERS**

- Choose four positive integers between 1 and 9.
  Say 3, 4, 7 and 9.

- If you make two 2-digit numbers out of these four digits, and multiply them together, what's the biggest product you can make?
  For example, $34 \times 79 = 2686$, but can you do better?

  Answer:
  The biggest product comes from $93 \times 74 = 6882$.
  If you have four digits $a < b < c < d$, then you always need to do "da"×"cb".
  The logic here is that you want to put the two biggest digits (d and c) in the tens columns, and then b (the next biggest digit) must go with c (not d) so that it gets multiplied by the d in the tens column of the other number.

- What if you're allowed to make a 3-digit number. You're still allowed only one multiplication sign. Will that get you a bigger product?

  Answer: No.

- What if you have five digits; say, 2, 3, 4, 7 and 9.
  What's the biggest possible product now? You can use 1-digit, 2-digit, 3-digit or 4-digit numbers, but you may use each digit only once and you are allowed only one multiplication sign.

  Answer:
  The biggest product now comes from $742 \times 93 = 69006$.
  If you have five digits $a < b < c < d < e$, then you need to do "dca"×"eb".
  The logic here is that you want to put the two biggest digits (c and d) in the highest possible columns, and then c (the next biggest digit) must go with d (not e) so that it gets multiplied by the e in the other number.

Extra Task

Using the digits 1, 2, 3, 4, 5, 6, 7, 8 and 9 and one multiplication sign only, what is the largest product you can make?
Answer: $87531 \times 9642 = 843973902$

Instant Maths Ideas: 3

Scoring 100

TEACHER'S NOTES AND ANSWERS

Making 100.

In pairs.

- Player 1 chooses an integer between 1 and 10 (inclusive) and writes it at the top of a piece of paper.
- Player 2 then chooses an integer (again, between 1 and 10 inclusive), adds it to the number on the paper and writes the answer below the number player 1 wrote.
- The players continue, taking it in turns.
- The winner is the first person to reach 100 exactly.

Play it a few times.
Can you work out a strategy so that you stand the best chance of winning.
Can you be sure of always winning?

The best strategy is always to add on whatever you need to to make one of these numbers:
1, 12, 23, 34, 45, 56, 67, 78 or 89 (the units digit is always one more than tens digit).
Once you've got to any one of these numbers, you're certain to win, so long as you keep with this strategy.

(The teacher can play this strategy and "beat anyone". "How am I doing it?" So as not to make it too obvious, you can take a risk and play randomly until you get to about 50.)

If the other person doesn't know about this strategy and you follow it, you will usually win. If you start, then you should certainly win.

Avoiding 100.

In pairs.

The same game as above, but this time whoever makes 100 *loses*. (You have to force the *other* person to make 100.)

When the strategy to the above game has been determined, change the rules to make it into this game.

This time the numbers you have to aim for are 1 less; i.e., 11, 22, 33, 44, 55, 66, 77, 88 or 99 (the eleven times table).

This time if the other person starts and you follow this strategy you should always win. This is a nice example of a situation where starting is a disadvantage. This happens because whatever number you start with, the other person (if they realise it) can always add on enough to make 11 (the first "magic number") and then keep with this strategy and win.

What if the target were not 100 but a different number?
Which "magic numbers" would you have to aim for along the way?

Broken Calculator   **TEACHER'S NOTES AND ANSWERS**

Imagine you have a simple non-scientific calculator, but it is broken.
The only buttons that will work are these ones:

$\boxed{3}$ $\boxed{4}$ $\boxed{-}$ $\boxed{\times}$ $\boxed{=}$

The calculator's insides are OK, and it still gives correct answers.
You can read the display without any problem.

Which integers between 1 and 20 can you make appear on the display?

Are any impossible?

no.	one possible route	no.	one possible route
1	4 − 3	11	3 × 3 × 3 − 4 − 3 − 3 − 3 − 3
2	4 × 3 − 4 − 3 − 3	12	3 × 4
3	3	13	4 × 4 − 3
4	4	14	3 × 3 × 3 − 4 − 3 − 3 − 3
5	4 × 3 − 4 − 3	15	3 × 3 × 3 − 3 − 3 − 3 − 3
6	3 × 3 − 3	16	4 × 4
7	4 × 4 − 3 − 3 − 3	17	3 × 3 × 3 − 4 − 3 − 3
8	4 × 3 − 4	18	3 × 3 × 3 − 3 − 3 − 3
9	3 × 3	19	3 × 3 × 3 − 4 − 4
10	4 × 4 − 3 − 3	20	3 × 3 × 3 − 4 − 3

There are many other possibilities.

Try it with different calculator buttons.

Are some buttons more "valuable" than others?

> *Clearly the +/− button or the subtract button is necessary if we're to get to any negative numbers.*

Instant Maths Ideas: 3

Day of the Week

Everyone knows their date of birth, but do you know which *day of the week* you were born on? If you don't, you can work it out; if you do, you can check that this process works.

When you do the divisions, always find an *integer* answer; ignore any remainder, and round *down*; so even if it's 19.8571... you give the answer 19.

Let's take Albert Einstein's birthday, 14 March 1879, as an example.

1. Start with the century number (e.g., 19 for 19-something, 20 for 20-something), and divide it by 4. Whatever the *remainder* is, call it r; so we have $18 \div 4 = 4$ remainder 2, so $r = 2$ for our date.

2. In the formula below,
   d = the day number; so $d = 14$;
   m = the month number (March = 3, April = 4, etc., except that January = 13 instead of 1 and February = 14 instead of 2); so $m = 3$;
   y = the year within the century (so it's between 0 and 99); so $y = 79$.

3. Now work out
$$A = d + \frac{26(m+1)}{10} + y + \frac{y}{4} + 5r;$$
   remembering with each division to round to the next integer *down*.

4. Now divide A by 7 and call the *remainder* x.

5. Convert x to the day of the week (Sunday = 1, Monday = 2, etc.)
   This is the day that we're after.
   So in our example we get
$$A = 14 + \frac{26 \times (14+1)}{10} + 79 + \frac{79}{4} + 5 \times 2$$
$$= 132 \text{ (rounding down)}$$
$$\frac{A}{7} = \frac{132}{7}$$
$$= 18\tfrac{6}{7}$$
   so $x = 6$ (Friday)

   which is correct.

Try this out on your birthday or on today's date to check that it works.

Puzzle
Decide which of the dates goes with which description:

"Black Friday"	1 May 1997
"Bloody Sunday"	16 September 1992
"Black Wednesday"	18 November 1910
UK General Election Day	22 January 1905

3.7 Spreadsheet Tasks

- When you have the opportunity to use a spreadsheet program, there are many good tasks you can do (see sheets). Some explanation of how a spreadsheet works may be needed, depending on pupils' previous experience, but the sheets are intended for pupils to work through relatively independently (e.g., in pairs) at their own speed.
- Pupils will need to know to use ***** for multiplication and **/** for division, and where to find them on the keyboard. The other necessary skill to teach at the beginning is how to copy a formula "down a column". (You could demonstrate how to put the numbers 1 to 20 into column A in just a few seconds.)

3.7.1 1. Think of a Number.
A fairly easy task to begin.

Answer:
The overall effect is to add 10.
$\frac{1}{4}(2(2(x+17)-4)-20)$
$= \frac{1}{4}(2(2x+30)-20)$
$= \frac{1}{4}(4x+40) = x+10$

3.7.2 2. How Old Are You?

Some pupils may expect the number to change every second (since a computer is a "live" thing and it ought to know that we're all getting older all the time), but the computer doesn't "know" that its sums have got anything to do with time.

Answer:
A thirteen-year-old (for example) should be about 4×10^8 seconds old.
10 years = 3×10^8
100 years = 3×10^9

You may need to show pupils how to widen the columns so that the numbers display properly. Standard form notation (with an E) can be confusing.

3.7.3 3. Magic Squares.
e.g.,

2	9	4
7	5	3
6	1	8

Answer:
There are many, but a 5 in the middle and even numbers in the corners will help. That way you can use all the integers from 1 to 9 once each and get a magic total of 15.

3.7.4 4. Sequences.
"Winning" means getting bigger faster.

Answer:
Higher powers will win!

3.7.5 5. More Sequences.

The nth term is given by the expression
$\frac{1}{3}(a+2b)+\frac{4}{3}(b-a)(-\frac{1}{2})^n$, and as $n \to \infty$, this expression $\to \frac{1}{3}(a+2b)$.
With $a=7$ and $b=3$, the nth term becomes
$\frac{13}{3}-\frac{16}{3}(-\frac{1}{2})^n$, which $\to 4\frac{1}{3}$ as $n \to \infty$.

Answer:
If a is the first number and b is the second, then the sequence gets closer and closer to $\frac{1}{3}a+\frac{2}{3}b$, so for 7 and 3 you should get $4\frac{1}{3}$.
Using 3 and 7 (the same starting numbers, but in the opposite starting order) gives $5\frac{2}{3}$.

3.7.6 6. Boxes.
A Fibonacci-type *(1170-1250)* investigation.

This idea also appears in section 3.6.18.

Answer:
Pairs of starting values that work are (2, 24); (7,21); (12,18); (17,15); (22,12); (27,9); (32,6) and (37,3). Algebraically we want solutions to $3x+5y=126$ where x and y are positive integers.

Instant Maths Ideas: 3

3.7.7	7. Credit Card Numbers.	*Answers:* a yes; b yes; c yes; d yes; e no.
3.7.8	8. Even More Sequences.	*Answer:* *If the first term is a and you divide by n each time, the sum gets closer and closer to $\frac{an}{n-1}$.* *So starting with 1 and dividing by 2 each time gives an infinite sum of 2.* *Starting with 1 and dividing by 3 each time gives an infinite sum of 1.5*
3.7.9	9. A Rich Aunt	*Answer:* (See the solution below.) *Which one you'd choose depends on how long you expect your Aunt to live (or whether she might change her mind before she dies!) and on how quickly you need the money!*
3.7.10	10. Cubic Graphs. *This is a task that you could do much more easily using graph-plotting software (see section 1.24.3). One advantage of this approach is to give some insight into how such programs actually work.*	*Answers:* *There are three basic types of cubic graph (plus their reflections in the y-axis):* - *like $y = x^3$, no peaks/troughs, gradient zero at the origin;* - *like $y = x^3 + x$, no peaks/troughs, gradient positive at the origin;* - *like $y = x^3 - x$, 1 peak and 1 trough, gradient negative at the origin.* *$y = 2^x$ grows the fastest for large enough x.*

Rich Aunt Solution (Task 9)

years	plan A	plan A total	plan B	plan B total	plan C	plan C total	plan D	plan D total
1	100	100	10	10	10.00	10.00	1	1
2	90	190	20	30	15.00	25.00	2	3
3	80	270	30	60	22.50	47.50	4	7
4	70	340	40	100	33.75	81.25	8	15
5	60	400	50	150	50.63	131.88	16	31
6	50	450	60	210	75.94	207.81	32	63
7	40	490	70	280	113.91	321.72	64	127
8	30	520	80	360	170.86	492.58	128	255
9	20	540	90	450	256.29	748.87	256	511
10	10	550	100	550	384.43	1133.30	512	1023
11	0	550	110	660	576.65	1709.95	1024	2047
12	−10	540	120	780	864.98	2574.93	2048	4095
13	−20	520	130	910	1297.46	3872.39	4096	8191
14	−30	490	140	1050	1946.20	5818.59	8192	16383
15	−40	450	150	1200	2919.29	8737.88	16384	32767
16	−50	400	160	1360	4378.94	13116.82	32768	65535
17	−60	340	170	1530	6568.41	19685.23	65536	131071
18	−70	270	180	1710	9852.61	29537.84	131072	262143
19	−80	190	190	1900	14778.92	44316.76	262144	524287
20	−90	100	200	2100	22168.38	66485.13	524288	1048575

1 Think of a Number

	A	B
1	Think of a Number Investigation	
2		
3	Starting number	
4	Add 17	
5	Double it	
6	Subtract 4	
7	Double it again	
8	Subtract 20	
9	Divide by 4	
10		
11		
12		
13		
14		
15		

- Start a new spreadsheet.
- Copy this writing into the spreadsheet.
- Think of a number and put it in cell B3.
  This is the starting number.
- Type the formula **=B3+17** into cell B4.
  This will work out the new number.
- Put the right formulas into cells B5-B9.
- Look at the number in cell B9.
  Compare it with the starting number.
- Change the starting number and see what happens to the number in B9.
  Write down what you notice.

Questions

Can you explain what is happening?
Try changing the formulas. What will happen to the number in B9?

2 How Old Are You?

	A	B
1	How Old Are You?	
2		
3	In years	
4	In weeks	
5	In days	
6	In hours	
7	In minutes	
8	In seconds	
9		
10		
11		

- Start a new spreadsheet.
  We are going to use a spreadsheet to work out how old you are – in seconds!
- Copy this writing into the spreadsheet.
- Put your age (in years) into cell B3.
- Type the formula **=B3*52** into cell B4.
  This will work out how many weeks you have been alive.
- Put the right formulas into cells B5-B8.
- Write down how many seconds you have been alive.

Questions

Use the spreadsheet to answer these questions.
    How many seconds is 10 years?
    How many more seconds do you think you will live?
    How many seconds are there in a century?

Instant Maths Ideas: 3

3 Magic Squares

	A	B	C	D
1	Magic Squares			
2				
3	1	5	2	
4	6	3	4	
5	8	7	9	
6				
7				

- Start a new spreadsheet.
  We are going to use a spreadsheet to make some *magic squares*.
  In a *magic square* the numbers in every row add up to the same total. The numbers in every column also add up to the same total, and the diagonal numbers also add up to the same total.

- Copy these numbers into the spreadsheet. This is **not** a magic square.
- Type the formula **=A5+B4+C3** into cell D2.
  This will work out the total for the 8,3,2 diagonal.
- Put a formula into cell D3 that will add up A3, B3 and C3 (the top row).
- Put formulas into D4 and D5 to add up the second and third rows.
- Put formulas into A6, B6 and C6 to add up the columns.
- Put a formula into D6 to add up the 1,3,9 diagonal.
  Now you can see all the totals around the edge of the number square.

Questions

How can you tell that this is not a magic square?
Change some of the numbers in the square. (Don't alter the formulas.)
The totals will change around the sides.
Can you make it into a magic square? *[Hint: Try making all the totals 15]*

4 Sequences

	A	B
1	Sequences	
2		
3	Counting	Triangle
4	1	1
5		
6		
7		
8		

- Start a new spreadsheet.
  We are going to use a spreadsheet to work out some *sequences*.
- In maths, a *sequence* is a list of numbers that follow a rule. The simplest one is the counting numbers: 1, 2, 3, 4, 5, and so on.
- Copy this writing into the spreadsheet.
- Put the formula **=A4+1** into cell A5.

- Copy this down to cell A23, so that you have the first 20 counting numbers.
  [You need to "click-and-drag": you may need to ask for help doing this.]
- In column B we are going to put a sequence of numbers called the *triangle numbers*.
  They are the "running total" of the counting numbers.
- In cell B5 put the formula **=B4+A5**.
- Copy this down to cell B23.
  These are the *triangle numbers*. Do you know why they are called triangle numbers?
  The sequence of *square numbers* have challenged the triangle numbers to a race!
  Square numbers are 1*1=1 and 2*2=4 and 3*3=9 and so on.
- Use the spreadsheet to put the first 20 square numbers (starting with 1) in column C.
  Do they beat the triangle numbers?
  Add an extra column for the *cube numbers* (powers of 3).
  They are 1*1*1=1 and 2*2*2=8 and 3*3*3=27 and so on.
  Which sequence of numbers wins?
  What do you think will happen if the powers of 4 and powers of 5 join in?
  Who will win now?

76 Instant Maths Ideas: 3

5 More Sequences

	A	B	C
1	More Sequences		
2			
3	1	7	
4	2	3	
5	3		
6	4		
7	5		
8	6		
9	7		
10	8		
11	9		
12	10		

- Start a new spreadsheet.
  We are going to try a more complicated sequence this time.
- Copy this writing into the spreadsheet.
- Make the counting numbers go down to cell A23 again.
  Remember to use the quick way of doing this.
- Put the numbers 7 and 3 into column B.
  They are the starting numbers.
  The rule for this sequence is that the next number is the *mean* of the last two.

The spreadsheet will work out the mean using the **AVERAGE** command.

- Put the formula =**AVERAGE(B3:B4)** into cell B5.
  [Note that you must put a colon **:** between the addresses of the two cells.]
  The answer should be 5 because 5 is the mean of 7 and 3. [Mean = (7+3)/2]
- Copy this formula down to cell B23.
  What happens to the numbers in the sequence?
  Try changing the 7 and 3 to different numbers. Can you work out what is going on?
  What have the final numbers got to do with the first two numbers that you choose?

6 Boxes

Here is a puzzle. Use a spreadsheet to help you solve it.
Look at the numbers in these boxes.

3	5	8	13	21	34

Going from left to right, each number is the sum of the *two* previous numbers.
3 + 5 = 8 and 5 + 8 = 13 and so on.

Suppose the final number is 126.

					126

Find 2 starting numbers that will give 126 in the final box.
For example, 10 and 12 won't do. They would make 90 in the final box (34+56).

10	12	22	34	56	90

Find out how many different pairs of numbers will make 126 in the final box.

How to do it

Set up a column in a spreadsheet to do all the adding up for you.
Every time you type in two starting numbers it does all the calculations, and you can see if you get to 126 at the end.
Be systematic with the numbers you try. Make sure you find *all* the solutions.

7 Credit Card Numbers

Many credit card numbers are 16 digits long. But not just any 16-digit number is a valid credit card number. There are some rules about what makes a valid credit card number. One simple one is this rule.

Take the 16 digits and number them from 1 to 16 from left to right.

1	2	3	4	5	6	7	8	9	10	11	12	13	14	15	16
4	0	4	9	4	0	3	2	1	6	7	2	3	1	0	7

Double every other digit, starting with the first. Write these in underneath.

8		8		8		6		2		14		6		0	

Where you end up with a 2-digit answer (like 14), add together the two digits (1+4=5).
Fill in all the other spaces with the original digits – you don't double these ones.

8	0	8	9	8	0	6	2	2	6	5	2	6	1	0	7

Add up the numbers you end up with. This one comes to 70.
A valid credit card number will always come to a multiple of 10 (10, 20, 30, etc.).

Design a spreadsheet to check if these numbers could be valid credit card numbers.

a	4	0	4	9	2	8	4	3	0	6	4	2	1	8	9	7
b	4	0	4	9	3	0	6	4	8	6	3	1	8	3	4	4
c	4	0	4	9	3	4	1	0	2	9	5	3	4	2	1	4
d	4	0	4	9	2	0	1	7	2	6	3	5	1	4	9	6
e	4	0	4	9	2	6	3	1	8	1	9	0	3	4	2	5

8 Even More Sequences!

This time you are going to use a spreadsheet to look at the sequence of numbers you get if you start with 1 and keep dividing by 2 each time to get the next number. It begins 1, 0.5, 0.25, …

- Put the first 20 terms into cells A1 to A20.
  [You need to put **1** into cell A1. Cell A2 will be **=A1/2** and then copy this formula down to A20.]

- Put a running total in cells B1 to B2.
  [Cell B1 will be **=A1**, B2 will be **=B1+A2**, and then copy this formula down to B20.]
  What number does the total of the sequence get closer and closer to?
  (Look at the numbers in B18, B19 and B20.)

- Try putting the number 12 into A1 instead of 1.
  What is the new total for the sequence?
  Try some other numbers in A1. What is the connection?

- What if you go back to starting with 1 but this time divide by *3* each time?
  Can you write the rule in algebra – if you started with *a* and divided by *n* each time what would the total be in algebra?

    Extra Task:
    Select cells A1-A20 and B1-B20 and click on the graph icon at the top.
    Choose line graph and put the graph into your spreadsheet.

9 A Rich Aunt

Your rich aunt sends you this letter:

Now that I'm getting on in years (I'm 70 today), I want to give you some of my money.
You can choose whether to have
A   £100 now, £90 next year, £80 the year after that, and so on;
B   £10 now, £20 next year, £30 the year after that, and so on;
C   £10 now, 1½ times as much next year, 1½ times as much as that the year after, and so on;
D   £1 now, £2 next year, £4 the year after, £8 the year after that, and so on.

Of course, the scheme will only run while I am alive!

Design a spreadsheet to work out how much money you would earn from each scheme in
  1   5 years
  2   10 years
  3   15 years

Which one would you choose?

10 Cubic Graphs

Cubic graphs are graphs of equations that contain an x^3 term (x to the power of 3).
In a spreadsheet the "to the power of" symbol is ^.

You are going to use a spreadsheet to calculate some values of functions involving x^3, and then use the graph feature to draw the graphs.

First we want some values of x^3, so we'll vary x between -2 and 2 and work out x^3 for each.
- In column A we want the x numbers from -2 to 2 going up in 0.2's.
  In cell A1 we need **–2** and in cell A2 **=A1+0.2**.
  Copy this formula down column A until you get to 2 (up to cell A21 if you start in A1).
- In column B we want the x^3 numbers. So in cell B1 the formula will be **=A1^3**. Copy this down column B (to cell B21).
- Now if you select columns A and B and click on the graph icon, you can see what the graph of $y = x^3$ looks like. Choose the scatter-graph option.
  Describe the shape of the graph.

Now try drawing some of these graphs.
How are they different from each other? How are they similar?
Where (at what value(s) of x) do they cross the x axis (horizontal one)?

$y = -x^3$ $y = x^3 + x$ $y = x^3 - x$ $y = 2x^3$ $y = x^3 + 2$

[You will need to use formulas like **=–A1^3** and **=A1^3+A1** and **=2*A1^3**.]

Extra Task:
Plot these graphs (below) for x between -5 and 5 and describe the ways in which they are different.
Although they all contain an x and a 2, they do not look alike.

$y = x + 2$ $y = 2x$ $y = x^2$ $y = 2^x$

Which one grows the fastest as x increases?

3.8 LOGO Tasks

- Although LOGO is quick to get the hang of, some pupils will find it much easier than others, perhaps because of spatial awareness and confidence with angles, or just because of general familiarity with computers.
- The best approach to "debugging" is to get a blank sheet of scrap paper and follow the instructions you've given the turtle yourself (or get someone else to). Do it carefully and you will often see where you've gone wrong.

3.8.1 People maths.
If pupils are not familiar with the principle of LOGO, choose someone to be "the turtle" and give them oral instructions; e.g., "Go forward 3 paces; turn 90° to your left"; etc., and so introduce the commands `FD`, `LT`, `BK`, `RT`.
`PU`, `PD` and `CS` can also be explained.

See sheet for the LOGO commands.

3.8.2 On the computers, easy tasks to begin with are to draw a square, then an equilateral triangle, then fill the screen with parallel lines.

Note the importance of a space in a command like `FD 100`.)

As soon as possible, pupils need to know about the `REPEAT` *command (there's no abbreviation for this one) so that they can progress to more complicated tasks without laborious work.*

For a closed polygon, you need to keep turning the same way; e.g., `LT` *(or* `RT`*) four times for a square. A common difficulty is not seeing that left and right get switched round when the turtle is coming down the screen.*

In drawing the equilateral triangle, some pupils are likely to use 60° instead of 120° as the angle and to end up with half a regular hexagon.
Imagining being the turtle yourself helps with seeing that it's the exterior *angle, not the interior angle, that the turtle turns through.*

3.8.3 Polygons and Circles.
Once `REPEAT` is understood, harder tasks are to draw other regular polygons.

Draw me a polygon with 360 sides.
What does it look like.

Draw a circle with half the diameter of that one.

Draw a circle that fits exactly *inside* a square, just touching each side.

Draw a circle that fits exactly *outside* a square, just touching each side.

This is much harder. One way is to draw the square and use Pythagoras' Theorem to calculate the length of its diagonal. Then use this as the diameter of the circle, using $c = \pi d$ *to find the circumference and dividing by 360.*

The `PENERASE` *mode soon comes in handy (rub-out-mode!). You get out of it by entering* `PD`.

A pretty decent-looking circle is produced by the command
`REPEAT 360 [FD 1 LT 1]`

`REPEAT 360 [FD 0.5 LT 1]`

The circumference of the first circle was about 360 units, and the second one 180 units.
So using $c = \pi d$ *, the diameter of the first must be about* $\frac{360}{\pi} = 115$ *units, so a square with sides this much will just enclose the circle.*

Alternatively, decide that the circle has to have twice the area of the previous one and scale up the steps round the outside in the ratio $1 : \sqrt{2}$ *;*
i.e., `REPEAT 360 [FD 1.41 LT 1]`.

3.8.4 Procedures.
The other important technique to use is procedures; e.g., if you enter

```
TO SQUARE
REPEAT 4 [FD 40 RT 90]
END
```

from then on, typing `SQUARE` will draw a square.

If you enter

```
TO SQUARE :SIDE
REPEAT 4 [FD :SIDE RT 90]
END
```

then typing `SQUARE 100` will draw a square with sides 100 units long.
Notice the colon before the word `SIDE` to indicate that it is a variable.

This is very much easier if pupils have some experience of computer programming in whatever language.

3.8.5 From this point on, you can have a range of challenges for pupils to attempt. One system is to draw them on an A3 sheet and stick it onto the wall.
Can you make this?
How "elegantly" can you program it?

See sheet for ideas.

Pupils should certainly aim to use procedures or **REPEAT** *for anything repetitive.*

3.8.6 Wallpaper.
An interesting project.

Pupils begin by making a procedure for their design, which could be a cross or a pentagram. Then they make a tessellation of a simple shape; e.g., a parallelogram. Finally, the challenge is to put these together, so that the turtle moves (pen up) along the sides of the tessellating shapes, drawing the design (pen down) at each vertex before pen-upping and moving on to the next vertex.

You can make beautiful designs this way.

3.8.7 Animations.

The idea here is to make a procedure for, say, a stick-person. The turtle draws this a certain number of times (so it lasts long enough for us to see it) before going **PENERASE** and drawing it once more. Then the turtle moves forward (or back or whatever) and goes **PD** and starts again.
The effect is that the object (with a bit of a flicker) moves across the screen.

Pupils can be highly ingenious with this technique, but it does take a reasonable amount of time.

LOGO Tasks

FD *forward*   BK *backward*

LT *left*   RT *right*

PU *pen up*   PD *pen down*

HT *hide turtle*   ST *show turtle*

CS *clear screen*   CT *clear text*

PENERASE *rub-out mode*   (PD *cancels this mode*)

Use the **REPEAT** command with square brackets like this; e.g., **REPEAT 4 [FD 40 RT 90]**
Use **TO** followed by a name to make a procedure, and finish with **END**.
If you want to make a variable, remember to put a colon (**:**) in front of it whenever you use it.

Here are some tasks to try:

1 Draw a straight road with a dashed white line down the middle.
Can you make it into a dual carriageway?
Add some houses along one side.

2 Draw a brick wall. Make sure that the vertical sides of each brick line up with the *middle* of the bricks above and below it.

3 Can you make a tessellation of hexagons, like in a bee-hive?

4 Can you draw a cube so that it looks 3-dimensional?

5 Choose a design from below and see if you can draw it using LOGO.

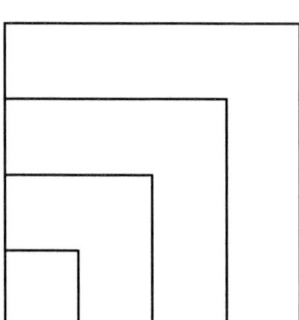

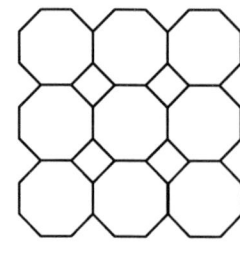

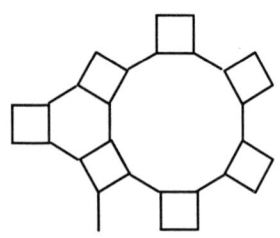

try continuing this tessellation

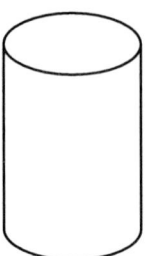

Instant Maths Ideas: 3

Mathematics Books and Websites

Books for General Interest
(This is very much a brief personal selection, and many good titles have been left out.)

A Mathematician Reads the Newspaper, John Allen Paulos, Penguin, 1995.
Does God Play Dice?, Ian Stewart, Penguin, 1989.
Game, Set and Math, Ian Stewart, Penguin, 1989.
Learning and Doing Mathematics (2nd Edition), John Mason, QED, 1999.
Mathematics for the Curious, Peter Higgins, OUP, 1998.
My Best Mathematical and Logic Puzzles, Martin Gardner, Dover, 1994.
The Code Book, Simon Singh, Fourth Estate, 1999.
The Golden Ratio, Mario Livio, Review, 2002.
The Penguin Book of Curious and Interesting Puzzles, David Wells, Penguin, 1992.
The Penguin Dictionary of Curious and Interesting Numbers, David Wells, Penguin, 1997.
Why Do Buses Come in Threes?, Rob Eastaway and Jeremy Wyndham, Robson, 1998.

Resources for the Classroom
(There are a lot of very helpful materials available from these sources; in particular, the regular magazines from ATM and MA.)

- ATM (*The Association of Teachers of Mathematics*)   http://www.atm.org.uk/
- MA (*The Mathematical Association*)   http://www.m-a.org.uk/
- *Tarquin Publications*   http://www.tarquin-books.demon.co.uk/math/newmathslist.html

Mathematics Websites

For Pupils and Teachers:

http://www.nrich.maths.org.uk/	an excellent site
http://plus.maths.org/index.html	an online maths magazine
http://www.cut-the-knot.org/content.shtml	lots of good material
http://www.trottermath.com/contents.html	fun maths puzzles and tricks
http://www.curiousmath.com/index.php	number tricks and puzzles
http://www.puzzlemaster.co.uk/Puzzle_panel/puzzle_panel_main.htm	various puzzles, not just maths
http://www.waldomaths.com/	good visual demonstrations
http://www.heymath.net/index.html	help when you're stuck
http://www.newton.dep.anl.gov/askasci/math98.htm	"ask a mathematician!"
http://www.bbc.co.uk/schools/gcsebitesize/maths/	GCSE revision site
http://www.bbc.co.uk/education/mathsfile/index.shtml	various games
http://mathforum.com/	lots of information
http://www.counton.org/	varied material
http://www.mathsfiles.com/	aimed at A-level
http://meikleriggs.co.uk/	aimed at A-level
http://integrals.wolfram.com/	integrates virtually anything!

Mainly for Teachers:

http://www.argonet.co.uk/oundlesch/mlink.html	many useful links
http://www.ex.ac.uk/cimt/	many useful resources
http://www.tes.co.uk/	*Times Educational Supplement*
http://www.mathsnet.net/	various
http://1000problems.com/	various
http://www.ies.co.jp/math/java/index.html	visual demonstrations
http://www.mathpages.com/home/	lots of information
http://www.ukmt.org.uk/	*UK Mathematics Trust* (organisers of national maths competitions)

Key Stage 3 Strategy – Key Objectives Index

These are the key objectives from the *Key Stage 3 Strategy* (DfES, 2001) with references to sections of relevant material from all three volumes.

Year 7

Simplify fractions by cancelling all common factors; identify equivalent fractions.	1.6
Recognise the equivalence of percentages, fractions and decimals.	1.11
Extend mental methods of calculation to include decimals, fractions and percentages.	1.2-11, 3.6
Multiply and divide three-digit by two-digit integers; extend to multiplying and dividing decimals with one or two places by single-digit integers.	1.5, 3.6
Break a complex calculation into simpler steps, choosing and using appropriate and efficient operations and methods.	various
Check a result by considering whether it is of the right order of magnitude.	1.15, 2.15-16
Use letter symbols to represent unknown numbers or variables.	1.19-22, 1.26
Know and use the order of operations and understand that algebraic operations follow the same conventions and order as arithmetic operations.	1.12, 1.20
Plot the graphs of simple linear functions.	1.23
Identify parallel and perpendicular lines; know the sum of angles at a point, on a straight line and in a triangle.	2.4-5
Convert one metric unit to another (e.g., grams to kilograms); read and interpret scales on a range of measuring instruments.	2.15, 1.2
Compare two simple distributions using the range and one of the mode, median or mean.	3.3
Understand and use the probability scale from 0 to 1; find and justify probabilities based on equally likely outcomes in simple contexts.	3.5
Solve word problems and investigate in a range of contexts, explaining and justifying methods and conclusions.	various

Year 8

Add, subtract, multiply and divide integers.	1.3, 3.6
Use the equivalence of fractions, decimals and percentages to compare proportions; calculate percentages and find the outcome of a given percentage increase or decrease.	1.9-11
Divide a quantity into two or more parts in a given ratio; use the unitary method to solve simple word problems involving ratio and direct proportion.	1.10
Use standard column procedures for multiplication and division of integers and decimals, including by decimals such as 0.6 or 0.06; understand where to position the decimal point by considering equivalent calculations.	1.2-3, 1.5, 3.6
Simplify or transform linear expressions by collecting like terms; multiply a single term over a bracket.	1.20
Substitute integers into simple formulas.	1.20
Plot the graphs of linear functions, where y is given explicitly in terms of x; recognise that equations of the form $y = mx + c$ correspond to straight-line graphs.	1.23
Identify alternate and corresponding angles; understand a proof that the sum of the angles of a triangle is 180° and of a quadrilateral is 360°.	2.4
Enlarge 2-d shapes, given a centre of enlargement and a positive whole-number scale factor.	2.12-13
Use straight edge and compasses to do standard constructions.	2.8
Deduce and use formulas for the area of a triangle and parallelogram, and the volume of a cuboid; calculate volumes and surface areas of cuboids.	2.2, 2.9-10
Construct, on paper and using ICT, a range of graphs and charts; identify which are most useful in the context of a problem.	1.23-25, 3.2, 3.7
Find and record all possible mutually exclusive outcomes for single events and two successive events in a systematic way.	1.5
Identify the necessary information to solve a problem; represent problems and interpret solutions in algebraic, geometric or graphical form.	various
Use logical argument to establish the truth of a statement.	various

Year 9

Add, subtract, multiply and divide fractions.	1.7-8
Use proportional reasoning to solve a problem, choosing the correct numbers to take as 100% or as a whole.	1.9-10
Make and justify estimates and approximations of calculations.	1.4, 2.15-16
Construct and solve linear equations with integer co-efficients, using an appropriate method.	1.18, 1.20
Generate terms of a sequence using term-to-term and position-to-term definitions of the sequence, on paper and using ICT; write an expression to describe the nth term of an arithmetic sequence.	1.19, 3.7
Given values for m and c, find the gradient of lines given by equations of the form $y = mx + c$.	1.23
Construct functions arising from real-life problems and plot their corresponding graphs; interpret graphs arising from real situations.	1.24-25, 3.2
Solve geometrical problems using properties of angles, of parallel and intersecting lines, and of triangles and other polygons.	2.1, 2.4-5
Know that translations, rotations and reflections preserve length and angle and map objects onto congruent images.	2.12-13
Know and use the formulas for the circumference and area of a circle.	2.3
Design a survey or experiment to capture the necessary data from one or more sources; determine the sample size and degree of accuracy needed; design, trial and if necessary refine data collection sheets.	3.1
Communicate interpretations and results of a statistical enquiry using selected tables, graphs and diagrams in support.	3.2-3
Know that the sum of probabilities of all mutually exclusive outcomes is 1 and use this when solving problems.	3.5
Solve substantial problems by breaking them into simpler tasks, using a range of efficient techniques, methods and resources, including ICT; give solutions to an appropriate degree of accuracy.	1.4, 3.7, various
Present a concise, reasoned argument, using symbols, diagrams, graphs and related explanatory text.	various

Year 9 (extension)

Know and use the index laws for multiplication and division of positive integer powers.	1.14
Understand and use proportionality and calculate the result of any proportional change using multiplicative methods.	1.9-10
Square a linear expression and expand the product of two linear expressions of the form $x \pm n$; establish identities.	1.20-21
Solve a pair of simultaneous linear equations by eliminating one variable; link a graphical representation of an equation or a pair of equations to the algebraic solution.	1.22
Change the subject of a formula.	1.20
Know that if two 2-d shapes are similar, corresponding angles are equal and corresponding sides are in the same ratio.	2.12
Understand and apply Pythagoras' theorem.	2.7
Know from experience of constructing them that triangles given SSS, SAS, ASA or RHS are unique, but that triangles given SSA or AAA are not; apply these conditions to establish the congruence of triangles.	2.12
Use measures of speed and other compound measures to solve problems.	2.16
Identify possible sources of bias in a statistical enquiry and plan how to minimise it.	3.1
Examine critically the results of a statistical enquiry and justify choice of statistical representation in written presentations.	3.1-3
Generate fuller solutions to mathematical problems.	various
Recognise limitations on the accuracy of data and measurements.	1.4

Text © Colin Foster 2003
Original illustrations © Nelson Thornes Ltd 2003

The right of Colin Foster to be identified as author of this work has been asserted by him/her in accordance with the Copyright, Designs and Patents Act 1988.

All rights reserved. The copyright holders authorise ONLY users of *Instant Maths Ideas for Key Stage 3 Teachers: Data, Numeracy and ICT* to make photocopies for their own or their students' immediate use within the teaching context. No other rights are granted without permission in writing from the publishers or under licence from the Copyright Licensing Agency Limited. Further details of such licences (for reprographic reproduction) may be obtained from the Copyright Licensing Agency Limited, of 90 Tottenham Court Road, London W1T 4LP.

Copy by any other means or for any other purpose is strictly prohibited without prior written consent from the copyright holders. Application for such permission should be addressed to the publishers.

Any person who commits any unauthorised act in relation to this publication may be liable to criminal prosecution and civil claims for damages.

Published in 2003 by:
Nelson Thornes Ltd
Delta Place
27 Bath Road
CHELTENHAM
GL53 7TH
United Kingdom

04 05 06 07 / 10 9 8 7 6 5 4 3 2

A catalogue record for this book is available from the British Library

ISBN 0 7487 8670 8

Page make-up by Colin Foster

Printed in Great Britain
by Antony Rowe